E. L. Wilsher.

56. Fot

10. Poplar Close
Silsoe:

Portrait of Elstow

Bedfordshire

by

Muriel M. Hart

PORTRAIT OF ELSTOW, BEDFORDSHIRE
Copyright © Muriel M. Hart 2000

ISBN 0-9539157-0-0

First published 2000 by
C&C Printers
4-6 Houghton Road
Bedford
Bedfordshire
MK42 9HQ

C & C Printers
Pub & Distribution.
Bedfordshire.
01234/360936.

Printed by

Contents

Pictorial Reference

Introduction

"Elstow. It is famous everywhere, and will live with the name of England because it is John Bunyan's village". So wrote Arthur Mee in 1939 in "The Counties of Bedford and Huntingdon, Homes of Bunyan and Cromwell".

It is also a village with which my family has been involved since the 1790's, although by coincidence 140 years earlier in 1653 John Bunyan and William Whitbread both joined John Gifford's congregation in Bedford on the same day.

Muriel Hart has been most assiduous in unearthing stories and events and characters connected with Elstow and I shall be surprised if even people who thought they knew their village do not find something new within these pages. By researching and writing this book, she has done a great service to her adopted village.

Sam Whitbread
Southill, February 2000

Preface

This is not a history of Elstow, as there are many books about the village and John Bunyan, but a little portrait of the village over the years.

How did I come to write such a book? - well briefly - when I retired as Clerk to the Elstow Parish Council after twelve years, the Parish Councillors kindly treated me to an evening dinner and during the evening the Councillors were reminiscing about the village. As a "new comer" I found it all very interesting and remarked that a book could be written about some of the changes over the years, and of course, a comment was made that it would be a new task for me - what a silly idea! However the idea stayed with me for the rest of the year. I eventually visited some residents in the village and from what I gleaned from them and with information obtained from the County Records Office and the Reference Library, etc., the notes mounted up and finally, two years later, I compiled this book, which I hope will be of interest to the reader. As will be appreciated, dates vary in different records but the details given are as accurate as possible.

I am greatly indebted to all those who have helped me in any way with this book - a challenge completed!

Muriel M. Hart
January 2000

Acknowledgements

I wish to thank the following:- Mr Samuel Whitbread, the Reverend R. Huband, the Reverend J. Tibbs, Bedfordshire and Luton Archives and Record Services, Departments of the Bedford Borough Council and Bedfordshire County Council, R. Bartram, D. Benson, E. Bowen, A. Chapman, A. F. Cirket, S. S. Clark, J. Collins, B. Crouch, J. Franks, D. W. F. Hall, V. Kumar, G. Lambourne, G. Markham, C. Marotta, R. Marotta, A. Park, A. Simmons, F. Stapleton, Mrs S. Anderson, Mrs M. Baron, Mrs M. Blundell, Mrs M. Brightman, Mrs Herbert, Mrs P. Keep, Mrs S. King, Mrs Langley, Mrs S. Myers, Mrs J. Pegg, Mrs L. Pestell, Miss F. Prole, Mrs F. Roberts, Mrs Toms, Mrs Watson, Mrs S. Williams, Mr & Mrs M. Hurley, Mr & Mrs Simmonds, Mr & Mrs F. Wagstaff and Mr & Mrs R. Worthington-Ellis.

The following books have also been a source of information:- The Bunyan Country, Festival of Britain 1951, Grace Abounding, Elstow Moot Hall, History of Bedfordshire, The Tinker of Elstow and Elstow Abbey Church Guidebook.

Some of the photographs have been taken by Mrs M. Brightman, Mrs S. King, John Hinson and C. Marotta, others have been loaned. Thanks to all concerned.

Elstow

Though bypassed by the A6, in the name of progress, the village of Elstow is rich in echoes of the past.

Some say there are ghosts abroad and this could well be, especially when there are old burial grounds, some ruins of the Norman Abbey and very old cottages. That apparition that glided slowly past, the eerie chilling feel in the room, a sudden muffled cry - was it an optical illusion, senses working overtime, a dream, or was it a ghost - who knows?

Elstow is about two miles south of Bedford and renowned for its connection with John Bunyan, the author of The Pilgrim's Progress.

Elstow is believed to be a Saxon name probably from Aellen's Stow meaning the homestead of one Aellen who settled in the area at one time. During local archaeological excavations some years ago an 8th century Saxon shaft of a stone cross was found which would indicate that there was a Christian settlement around at that time. The Domesday Book has the name Elneston, the name being a debased form of Helenstowe, that is Helen's Place and derived from the dedication of a very early Church to St. Helena. However the village received its name it has been known as Elstow for centuries.

The Whitbread family have been associated with Elstow for over two hundred years. They purchased much of Elstow from the Hillersden family in 1792. The present Samuel Whitbread, who is a patron of the Elstow Abbey Church and Her Majesty's Lord Lieutenant of Bedfordshire, still owns a substantial amount of land and property in Elstow.

As well as houses and cottages owned by the Whitbread Estate, Elstow has private residences and some houses and flats owned by Housing Associations. There are a number of properties of architectural and historic interest dating from the 17th century or earlier.

Most villages had their craftsmen, such as carpenters, blacksmith and baker, Elstow was no exception, and it was also well known for lace making. Rushes used to be strewn on the floors of the cottages and around 1628 an

Elstow man started weaving rushes into mats, while at about the same time baskets were made from rushes gathered from the Elstow brook. Watch straps were also made in Elstow and it is known that there was a cooper and a joiner in the village too.

The Parish boundary is slightly different from the Ecclesiastical boundary. The Parish boundary stretches from the High Street in the north, eastwards to Medbury Farm, then south towards the Elstow Storage Depot and back westwards to what is known as "Race Meadows" near the Interchange Retail Park and the Hillersden estate; whereas the Ecclesiastical boundary includes the south side of Mile Road.

The Conservation Area covers the High Street from the St. Helena Restaurant and includes the Red Lion, Bunyan's Mead, the Moot Hall and the Green, along with the Elstow Abbey Church and lower part of West End.

The population of Elstow has grown steadily from 513 in 1931 to 608 in 1991 and 1200 in 1998.

There are about half a dozen people in the village who were born and bred in Elstow and have lived in the village all their lives.

Mr Richard Payne represents Elstow on the Bedfordshire County Council and Mr Martin Parker on Bedford Borough Council. Since 1997 the Member of Parliament for Mid-Bedfordshire has been Mr Jonathan Sayeed.

Elstow like many other villages throughout the country has changed over the years and unfortunately it seems that there are many more changes to come - they call it progress!

Chapter 1

ELSTOW ABBEY CHURCH

The focal point of the village is the Abbey Church of St. Mary and St. Helena which was originally part of a Benedictine Abbey. The Church is of historic and architectural interest.

The Benedictine Abbey was founded around 1080 by Judith, the niece of William the Conqueror, as an act of atonement for the execution of her husband Waltheof, a Saxon and Earl of Northumberland, whose connection with a plot against the King, Judith had inadvertently disclosed.

The Abbey which was built of stone acquired from Turvey stood near a stream, later to be known as Elstow Brook, and this was an advantage as it provided the necessary water for the nuns. Fishponds were dug nearby so that the nuns could have fish for their meals on Fridays. The building was in the Norman style and a later extension to the west was Early English. The Abbey was dedicated to Our Lady and the Holy Trinity and about a couple of centuries later a Chapel was built in the churchyard of the Abbey by Ivota and this was dedicated to St. Helena and was used by the parishioners for services so as not to inconvenience the Abbess and nuns. Licence for services was given by Thomas Bishop of Lincoln in 1345.

There are several traditions about St. Helena and it is difficult to know which one is true, suffice it to say that she was born at Drepanum in Asia Minor around 247, she married Constantius Chlorus and was mother of Constantine the Great. St. Helena became a Christian late in life and visited the Holy Land. Her name is particularly associated with the finding, near Mount Calvary, of the True Cross of Jerusalem. She died about 330. St. Helena's Feast Day is 18th August.

Although the Abbey did not fall under the Act of Dissolution in 1536 it surrendered in 1539 when the Abbess and remaining twenty-three nuns were granted pensions. At the time of the Dissolution the property of the Abbey was considerable; it was the eighth wealthiest and one of the largest Benedictine nunneries of the 106 which existed at the Dissolution. The land and property passed to the King who eventually conferred it upon Sir Humphrey Radclyff, brother of the Earl of Sussex, and his wife Dame Isabel. They lived in part of the convent until Sir Humphrey's death in 1566. Both Sir Humphrey and Sir Edward Radclyff were, in their day, Sheriffs of Bedford. There is a Radclyff memorial in the Church above the altar. This is unique as it portrays Sir Humphrey and Dame Isabel in a kneeling position facing each other.

About fifty years later, in 1616, Sir Humphrey's heirs sold the property to Sir Thomas Hillersden, who built a mansion from some of the materials of the Abbey, part of which had been demolished in 1580. Sir Thomas Hillersden became Lord of the Manor of Elstow, a title inherited by the first Samuel Whitbread when he purchased Hillersden Manor in 1792. Hillersden Manor was obviously a very large house, as when it became a ruin over the years the children of the village used to play in the ruins and often lost their way in the mass of rooms and corridors. The few remaining ruins, mostly covered in ivy, can be seen to the south side of the Church. A carriageway from the High Street used to cross the field by the Swan Public House to the Manor. The Hillersden family gave a Communion set to the Church and a memorial tablet to Thomas Hillersden, grandson of Sir Thomas, can be seen in the south aisle of the Church.

In 1580 the Abbey, once thought fit to be a cathedral, was partially destroyed by the demolition of the east end of the nave and all the Church further to the east. However, part of the Norman nave survived and thus the Abbey Church of St. Mary and St. Helena became the Church to serve the village of Elstow. The Church was extensively restored in 1880, the Whitbread family paying for the complete restoration. The work took two years to complete and the Church re-opened in May 1882 when the Vicar was the Reverend J. Copner. Over the years various repairs and improvements, both inside and out, have been undertaken.

On Easter Tuesday, 11th April 1882 a sale of useful and fancy items was held in the school to provide funds towards stained glass windows for the Church as a memorial to John Bunyan. The windows were installed at the east end of the south and north aisles during the restoration of the Church and depict scenes from The Pilgrim's Progress and The Holy War.

The Pilgrim's Progress window is in the Chapel situated in the south aisle of the Church and known as the Bunyan Chapel. Around 1928 the Church

Elstow Abbey Church   *Photo by C. Marotta*

Church Interior   *Photo by J. Hinson*

Hillersden Manor Ruins (*see page 12*)   *Photo by C. Marotta*

Lectern Carving of John Bunyan

Photo by J. Hinson

obtained a new altar, and altar rails were given by the Prole family. The old altar rails which were used in John Bunyan's time were naturally put into the Bunyan Chapel. The oak reredos, which was designed by the famous architect Sir Albert Richardson, was given by the Bedfordshire Branch of the Far Eastern Prisoners of War Association as a memorial to those prisoners who died in captivity in the Far East in 1941-1945. The dedication of the memorial took place on 5th May 1957. A former Vicar of Elstow, the Reverend Peter Hartley, and others associated with the parish, were prisoners of war in the Far East. The Bedfordshire Branch of the Far Eastern Prisoners of War hold their annual service of prayer and remembrance in the Church in June. A wreath of poppies is laid on the altar of the Chapel every Remembrance Sunday by a representative of the Far Eastern Prisoners of War (FEPOW).

Also in the south aisle, on the floor behind the choir stalls, are two brasses. One is of the Abbess, Elizabeth Harvey who died in 1527. This is a special brass as it shows the Abbess with her crozier; there are only two such brasses in the country. The other brass is of Dame Margery, who died in 1427, and was grandmother of Elizabeth Harvey. As the brasses were becoming rather worn and faint due to being walked over in past years, they have now been roped off to protect them.

The Chapel in the north aisle has been made into a Prayer Chapel. The stained glass window in this Chapel is of The Holy War. The oak altar was given through a faculty in 1922 by the old Elstow County School. The Prayer Chapel has been dedicated to the memory of the late Reverend Peter Hartley who was Vicar from 1953 to 1976 having succeeded his father the Reverend Victor Stanley Hartley, the Vicar from 1919 to 1953.

The two stained glass windows at the east end of the chancel were given in 1887 by the Wigram family in memory of their parents Tabitha who died in 1863 and Octavius who died in 1878. The glass was prepared in Germany by Meyer, celebrated artists of Munich and London and shows to the left the Adoration of the Wise Men and on the right the Ascension of Christ.

On the Church wall above the vestry door is a memorial in marble from the old Elstow County School (previously known as the Bedford County School) which was given to the Church in 1922. The memorial commemorates the old scholars of the school who died in the Great War. It is understood that the Bedford County School which opened in 1869 was a middle class public school and had pupils aged from nine to eighteen. The school was situated on

Ampthill Road where Granada now stands and in 1907 became known as Elstow County School although actually sited in Kempston. The school was run by Charles Farrar (born 1860) as a private school from 1893 until it closed in April 1916 when it was requisitioned as a Military College. It was eventually sold to Cosmic Crayon Company in 1920. Around 1902 an Old Boys Association, known as the Old Elstonians was formed. When the Association was wound up there were some reserves of cash and Government War Stock which were given to the then Vicar on condition that two wreaths be placed either side of the memorial on Remembrance Sunday. The wreaths to have blue and white ribbons, the colours of the Association. In 1933 the sports cups from the old school were given to the Church and were used to form the silver gilt cross which sometimes adorns the altar, in memory of Charles Farrar. Two silver gilt candlesticks were made to match the cross in memory of John Prole who was a churchwarden for forty years.

The perpendicular font in which John Bunyan was baptised in 1628 and his daughters in later years, dates from around the 13th century. It has been moved twice, as it was originally in the north aisle but during the restoration of the Church was moved into the south aisle. About eighty years later it was returned to its original position in the north aisle near the north doorway. This doorway is an exact copy of the old Norman doorway.

The Church used to be lit by gas mantles before electric lighting was installed with lights being suspended from the ceiling of the nave. However, within the last decade this old lighting has been replaced by a more modern style.

Heating the Church is quite an expensive item as it is such a large building. In past years the verger lit the boilers in the Church at 6 p.m. on a Saturday night and re-stoked them at midnight and again early on the Sunday morning, so that it was warm for the morning services. In the 1950s oil fired heating was installed in the old furnaces and latterly, because the choir stalls seemed to be exceptionally chilly, electric heaters were installed to help keep the choir warm. On cold days free standing oil heaters are used around the Church for weekday services.

The present Church organ, which was installed in 1939 and replaced an old one-manual barrel organ which had been converted in 1868, was refurbished in 1992.

Over the last decade an amplifying system has been installed in memory

The Font
Photo by J. Hinson

The Abbey Seal
(see page 19)

Photo by J. Hinson

Vaulted Roof of the Vestry

Tragedy in 1970
(see page 25)

of the late Jim Keep who was a staunch member of the Church and whose wife and daughter still live in the village. The hymn book cupboard at the back of the Church has been replaced with a new built-in bookcase and the Book of Remembrance is now housed in a glass topped case in the south aisle. Both these items have been presented to the Church in memory of Church members.

As candle grease from the lit candles on the altar was spoiling the altar cloth, imitation oil filled candles now adorn the altar. The Church was recarpeted in 1998.

Many more parents with young children now attend the Church, especially the Family Communion and the Young Peoples' services, so a small children's corner and play area have been created at the back of the Church.

The Abbey Church has a small choir of which one stalwart member is over 80 years of age and has been in the choir for over forty-five years.

A Service of Commemoration was introduced in 1997 and is usually held in November. Those who have been bereaved are able to ask for the names of those they have lost to be remembered. This is one of the best attended services in the year.

Outside the Church over the west door is a carved copy of the Common Seal of the Abbey that was used on the Deed of Surrender in 1539. It shows the Blessed Virgin holding the infant Holy Child and St. Helena holding a cross. Kneeling beneath are an Abbess with a crozier and two nuns.

Near the west door is a small door, now boarded up but still possessing it's original oak door with strap hinges. The postern in this door is the one immortalised by John Bunyan as the wicket gate in The Pilgrim's Progress when Christian fled for refuge.

The Vestry, which was a school room in John Bunyan's day, is situated in the south west corner of the Church and is entered by a small door down steps into a 13th century square vaulted room. The vestry has a fine vaulted roof which is supported by a central pillar of Purbeck marble, and has a very old stained glass window. Years ago a fire used to be lit in the fireplace on a Sunday to warm the vestry. In 1991 the flat roof of the vestry was replaced with a pitched roof, and a french ditch was dug round the outside of the vestry to alleviate dampness.

The detached Bell Tower which was built in the 13th century, was restored in 1965. Six bells are housed in it, one is known as the Bunyan Bell as it is reputed that John Bunyan used to ring the bell. The bells are rung regularly for

Sunday morning and evening services, for weddings, if required, and on other specific occasions. The Church is a popular venue for young bell ringers as the bells are well maintained, so often bell ringers from other Churches visit Elstow to ring a peal of bells, which takes about two and a half hours.

The clock on the bell tower was last restored in 1994 and has to be wound by hand.

The Churchyard used to extend to the Green and contains some very old gravestones. John Bunyan's mother, father and sister are buried in the churchyard but the exact position is not recorded. The churchyard wall was built in 1892. Some of the older trees have a preservation order on them so planning permission is required before any lopping of the trees, to safeguard the Church and churchyard, is undertaken. There is a Garden of Remembrance inside the main gate and more memorial stones are alongside the east wall of the churchyard.

As the churchyard is nearly full, Church officials are grateful to Mr Samuel Whitbread for giving, in 1998, a portion of the late Mr Charlie Prudden's garden as an extension.

The Diocese of St. Albans, like some other dioceses, have a ruling that no artificial flowers be allowed on graves. This is, of course, upsetting for some relatives but such flowers can become very tatty after facing the elements for a while and this can give the churchyard a rather unkempt and untidy appearance.

Keeping the churchyard neat and tidy is the duty of the Church caretaker, but at least once a year a Church working party spends a busy Saturday giving the churchyard a good tidy up.

The Vicarage which is situated at the top of Church End was built in 1966 on the tennis courts of the old vicarage. The old house, which dates from 1796, still stands alongside the present vicarage and is now a private residence.

There have been various archaeological investigations around the Church and village over the last four decades. Between 1965 and 1970 excavations on the Abbey site saw one hundred and fifty trenches dug by students, local sixth form pupils and other personnel. Although the work was hard and painstaking Roman-British coins and pottery were found and Saxon skeletons in a burial ground over which the original Abbey was built. A Saxon Cross Shaft of the late 8th century was also discovered, this is now in the Moot Hall. In the monastic graveyard near the east end of the Church a skeleton of a priest with a chalice was unearthed and a 14th century kitchen post was found. Drawings of the lay-out of the Church and Convent buildings are on display in the Church.

The Ecclesiastical boundary covers a wider area than the Civil Parish and takes in the south side of Mile Road as far as the John Bunyan School. The Church congregation comes, not only from Elstow, but Kempston, Wilstead and Bedford itself.

Over the years all kinds of events have taken place in the Church from special services to flower festivals and concerts. The list is endless and far too long to record here. However, thinking of just the last two decades maybe one or two events could be mentioned, such as the Concert of Classical Music by the Young People of Elstow Abbey Church performed one evening in September 1986. Nine performers took part and there was solo singing, piano and flute playing.

In Bedfordshire in 1988 to commemorate the tercentenary of the death of John Bunyan (in 1688) several events took place all through the year. Representatives from all walks of life and the Council of Churches joined together to make an enjoyable and memorable year and Elstow was one of the villages which took part.

On Saturday 2nd July a Vanity Fayre was held on the Elstow Green as a re-creation of an Elstow Fayre as John Bunyan would probably have known it. An Ecumenical Service was held in the Church on 31st August. This date is in the Church of England Calendar as John Bunyan Day. In September there was a Bell Ringer's service in the Church along with a Flower Festival with the theme "Harvest in John Bunyan's Time", but the highlight of events as far as Elstow was concerned was the production of Son-et-Lumière - a dramatic history of Elstow Abbey in sound and light. This took place in the Church on four evenings in October and was in aid of the Church Restoration Fund. Tickets were £1 and £2. The script writer and producer was a local school teacher (Mrs Jill Manning) and the co-ordinator was the Reverend John Tibbs, then Vicar of Elstow. About forty local people, including the Elstow Church choir and some boys from Bedford Modern School took part. After rehearsals and recordings in the Church, BBC Radio Bedfordshire kindly agreed to assist with some technical problems in the recording of the dramatic scenes. The cast spent most of one weekend at the Lurke Street Studios where recordings were made and compiled under the direction of Colin Burbridge. Hunting Engineering sponsored the event, electricity used in the performances was donated by the Eastern Electricity Board and the Marianettes of Bedford arranged the lighting and kindly loaned some of their equipment, the necessary scaffolding for the lights was provided by Dee Bee Scaffolding.

The whole performance was excellent and most enjoyable, the lighting and sound effects were most impressive. All performances were well attended and it is hoped that the audiences appreciated all the hard work that had gone into this production.

In May 1990 Elstow Abbey Church welcomed the Fredonia School of Music from the State University of New York College at Fredonia with their orchestra and Chamber Singers who were on a concert tour of Great Britain and Germany. The orchestra was conducted by Donald Lang, Professor of Music at the State University. The Chamber Singers had a reputation as one of America's finest collegiate choral ensembles. The evening programme featured a great variety of choral works from the Renaissance to Jazz. The members of the orchestra and choir stayed two nights with Church members whilst visiting Elstow, Woburn and Chicksands.

It is hoped that enjoyable and memorable events, such as musical evenings by the Bedfordshire Police Choir, will continue to be held in the Church for years to come.

Around 1985 in an endeavour to persuade more people to attend the Church a scheme was launched known as Outreach. Six to eight people met in homes of Church members one evening a week for six weeks and as well as religious discussion, ideas were suggested which might entice people to Church. From one of these meetings a social evening every so often for parishioners and friends was proposed. A small Committee was set up and the St. Helena Guild was formed. The Guild met once a month to begin with and had speakers from various organisations, held whist-drives, had mystery coach trips and even a night at the Proms in London. The activities were well attended and eventually meetings became fortnightly, with hindsight this was probably not a good idea as it became difficult to obtain speakers etc. The Guild began to organise fund raising activities and assisted with refreshments for other Church events, but as happens so often, over the years the faithful few were left to cope and gradually the Guild folded after five years.

A few years after the St. Helena Guild ceased, the Friends of Elstow Abbey Church was formed. This is a Registered Charity which organises popular functions to raise money for the upkeep of the church.

For decades St. Albans Abbey has held a Special Youth Service on Easter Monday afternoon. This is an Easter Pilgrimage for the Churches in the diocese and some people walk quite long distances to the Abbey. For a number of years many of the the younger members of Elstow Abbey Church, along with a few older members, walked from Elstow to St. Albans. The "pilgrims" used to leave the Church after the 9.30 a.m. service and walk to Luton where they stayed overnight in St. Mary's Church Hall. How much sleep they had is anyone's guess as there would be members of other Churches there too. They continued on their way to St. Albans bright and early on Easter Monday morning. There were, of course, for the length of the pilgrimage, back up cars with drinks, and plasters for blisters. Elstow "pilgrims" had a very decorative banner which was created by Margaret Anne Tibbs, the wife of the then Vicar, this was carried on the way. It can still be seen in the Church. Once at St. Albans it was time for lunch - soup and sandwiches supplied from the back up cars - then with banners held aloft the "pilgrims" from all the Churches processed into the Abbey for a wonderful, uplifting service of praise and thanksgiving. No doubt the older people who have been privileged to be present at one of these services would be quite overwhelmed by the reverence shown by the youth of the day. The return to Elstow was in the relative comfort of cars! Unfortunately, times change and for the past two or three years the pilgrimage from Elstow has not been undertaken, though some members of the Church have attended the service but have travelled by easier means on the day.

Elstow Abbey Church used to have a flourishing Youth Club but unfortunately a few years ago the chief leader moved and gradually the Youth Club ceased to function. Despite attempts to restart it this has proved unsuccessful, mostly due to lack of leaders. Whilst the Youth Club was in existence it had many lively discussions and undertook a variety of activities. On one occasion it was decided to hold a dinner party for twenty elderly folk from the village and as they wished to serve the meal in a professional way, the Youth Club sought assistance from a Bedford Hotel and the assistant manager, who had trained at Claridges Hotel in London, kindly provided the necessary tuition. The evening was a great success and it would seem that there is more to serving a dinner party than most people think.

The Elstow Youth Club took about sixteen members with eight leaders to Taize in 1985 in two cars and the Diocesan minibus. Two nights camping were spent in France on the way, and on the return journey, and three nights at Taize where all joined in worship and other events over a weekend with thousands of young people from all over the world.

The Sunday School has unfortunately met with difficulties over the years and has not been a continuous part of Church life. However in 1999 a Sunday School restarted but it seems that the words "Sunday School" are regarded as somewhat old fashioned so there are now Squirrels and Woodpeckers. Maybe these names will encourage children between the ages of two and ten years to attend Church at 9.30 a.m. twice a month and see what fun a Sunday lesson can be.

The cost of maintaining the Church and the Ministry is in the region of £85 a day. Through the generous giving of Church members, the financial position is fairly strong, thus enabling the Church to give at least ten per cent of its income to the work of missions and charities at home and abroad.

The Church has many visitors from near and far. Unfortunately the Church can not be left open as in years past, but the sexton, or Vicar if available, are always pleased to arrange access.

The Reverend Richard Huband has been the Vicar of Elstow since 1991 and the present churchwardens have both served the Church for over twenty years.

An old lamp barn stood to the south west of the Church and in 1968 War Stock was sold and used to remodel the barn into two toilets, a kitchen and an entrance foyer. A new building in the adjacent field formed a Church room and was later extended and made into the present Church Hall by Michael Hurley, a well known builder in the village. The kitchen and toilets were renovated in 1997, and paving slabs were laid from the Church to the Church Hall which made a great improvement from the grass path which became wet and muddy in inclement weather. The Church Hall is used by the Sunday School, and is in general use for meetings, jumble sales, bazaars etc. It can also be hired out for special functions.

CHURCH END

The road to the Church from the High Street is known as Church End. There is a small car park owned by the Church which was last resurfaced around 1996. Quite often the car park is not large enough and cars have to park outside the Vicarage and alongside the churchyard wall. At times, especially on Christmas Eve, Remembrance Sunday and for large Weddings, cars have to park on the High Street and even in the Red Lion car park by courtesy of the Manager.

Until 5th November 1970 a row of four picturesque thatched cottages, with big gardens, stood at the top of Church End where the Abbey Close flats now stand. Each cottage was double fronted, with the main bedroom downstairs. Unfortunately on that evening the thatch of one of the cottages caught fire from a stray firework and fire quickly spread through the hollow undivided roof space of the four cottages. The residents lost practically everything as articles which were recovered from the ground floors were so sodden by the water from the fire engines they were irreparable. The cottages had been built in 1798 by the second Samuel Whitbread who had inherited the estate from his father two years earlier.

The cottages had stood for two centuries but after the fire, as only the fragile shells remained, restoration was not feasible. Fortunately, there was no loss of life or injuries to the residents, all of whom were rehoused in the village. One of the tenants and her daughter still live in the village.

There are only three thatched cottages left in the village, one on the High Street and two on Wilstead Road.

Also on Church End, towards the south side of the Church are three very old cottages, which centuries ago were one dwelling and probably accommodated some of the residents of the old Abbey. Today one is occupied by a market trader dealing in eggs, fruit and vegetables. The barge board at the back of this cottage is elaborately decorated and there is a small model of a pig on the front of the roof. At one time a florist lived in the middle cottage and there was a large beehive in the garden. For the last fifty years the cottage has been inhabited by the sextons of the Church. It has a lovely garden and the present sexton opens it to the public on occasions for charity fundraising.

Chapter 2

THE ELSTOW GREEN

To the north of the Church is the Green which would have been part of the Abbey grounds. The Moot Hall stands on the Green. Since 1792 the Green has been owned by the Whitbread estate but was given over to Bedfordshire County Council in 1951 along with the Moot Hall. The Green is now owned and maintained by the County Council who have to grant permission for any activities to take place thereon.

It is reputed that John Bunyan used to play a game called Tipcat on the Green. This was a game similar to rounders where a small piece of wood similar to a cricket bail had to be hit into the air with a piece of wood or stout stick from a hole in the ground then hit again as it rose. In his unregenerate days John Bunyan recalls in Grace Abounding how as he "was in the midst of a game of cat, and having struck it one blow from the hole, just as I was about to strike it the second time a voice did suddenly dart from heaven into my soul, which said, wilt thou leave thy sins and go to heaven, or have thy sins and go to hell? At this I was put to an exceeding maze; wherefore, leaving my cat upon the ground, I looked up to heaven, and was, as if I had with the eyes of my understanding, seen the Lord Jesus looking down upon me, as being very hotly displeased with me, and as if he did severely threaten me with some grievous punishment for these and other my ungodly practices."

Markets and fairs were held regularly and there was a Charter by Henry II whereby the nuns of the Abbey could hold a Fair for four days at the beginning of May to help their finances, later a Fair was allowed in November. Traders, sellers and buyers travelled from afar for these markets and fairs which included the sale of cattle, horses and a variety of goods. The cattle, of course, having to be driven up the High Street to the Green. It is recorded that the gentry purchased articles for their homes from the fairs. Traders kept their takings in small chests and used to hire a man to look after them, but on one occasion £117 was stolen. In November 1678 a booth at the fair was broken into

The Green   *Photo by C. Marotta*

Old Cottages and Stump

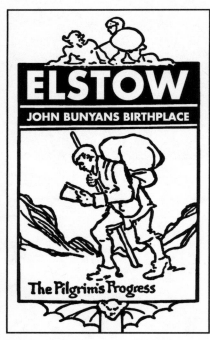

Village Sign 1920 Design

Village Sign 1989 (see page 31)

Photos by C. Marotta

and some hats stolen, the culprit received a gaol sentence for the offence. Although during the 19th century the markets and fairs gradually declined a local newspaper dated 20th May 1882 reported "that the annual cattle and pleasure fair had been held on Elstow Green" and in fact cattle fairs continued twice a year until the First World War. The pleasure fairs went on until the 1930s.

The stump of the old market cross can still be seen on the Green. At one time horses were allowed to graze on the Green for a fee, cows grazed thereon during the last war and goats have also been tethered on the Green.

A number of Village Greens have a road through the middle but this is not so at Elstow, though there is a pedestrian entrance from West End through a wooden clapping gate. Small thatched cottages used to face the Green.

It is understood that in the First World War there was a cookhouse and reception tent on the Green which was used by soldiers who were billeted in the area. In the last war there was a sandbagged gun implacement on the Green, and there were some slit trenches, dug by Italian Prisoners of War, in a field in front of the Church.

Over the years various activities have taken place on the Green as well as the May Festivals. Around 1920 a Caravan Mission to Village Children visited Elstow and had a tent on the Green for a week or so where services were held for children. This event was a great favourite with the local children.

In 1928 an inter-denominational service was held on the Green to mark the tercentenary of John Bunyan's birth. In May 1972 to celebrate the Golden Jubilee Year of the Rotary Club in Bedford and to mark the tercentenary of John Bunyan's release from prison on 9th May 1672, a mail coach visited the Green and souvenir envelopes were stamped and posted for a fee of five pence.

To celebrate the tercentenary of the publication of The Pilgrim's Progress in 1678, the Sealed Knot performed a re-enactment of a battle between Royalists and Roundheads on the Green in July 1978. Musketeers, Pikemen and small cannon were all in evidence in the demonstration of 17th century warfare. There was a display of militia drilling, and scenes from a 17th century Fair including morris dancing and wrestling.

The Sealed Knot Society takes its name from a royalist secret society who plotted during the commonwealth (1649-1660) for restoration of the monarchy. Members of the Sealed Knot are all volunteers and are organised on military lines. The Sealed Knot has two aims:- to arouse interest in and help research into the English Civil War period; and to help raise money for charity.

In 1988 a Bunyan Festival, promoted by Bedfordshire County Council to celebrate the life of John Bunyan (1628-1688) was held throughout Bedfordshire with various events taking place during the year. Elstow held a Vanity Fayre on the Green on 2nd July 1988 to mark the occasion. The stall holders dressed in 17th century costume and the afternoon's programme included maypole dancing and a pig roast. The Abbey Middle School performed informal scenes and happenings relating to the 17th century whilst pupils from John Bunyan Upper School presented Pressganging, Christian in a Cage and John Bunyan preaching and his arrest. The Sealed Knot also presented an encampment showing glimpses of Army conditions during the Civil War.

A John Bunyan and 17th century Festival was held in Bedford from 7th to 11th June 1995 as part of the town's contribution to the British Tourist Authority's nationwide Festival of Arts and Culture. The Festival was supported by Terry Waite who spoke at the service held in the Bunyan Meeting (Mill Street) on the Sunday at the close of the Festival. There were about twenty events around Bedford and the residents of Elstow, with the assistance of various organisations, staged another Vanity Fayre which included circus acts and falconry. Although well attended it was not on such a large scale as in 1988.

There are some old chestnut trees on the Green and the old vicarage overlooks the Green. The oak tree near the Moot Hall was planted in 1960 by Councillor R. Hoburn, the Chairman of the County Records Committee, in connection with the exhibition held in the Moot Hall that year concerning the restoration of Charles II to the throne in 1660. It was a sapling from the original Boscobel oak tree in which Charles II is reputed to have hidden in 1651 following the battle of Worcester.

As a sign of the times a dog waste bin has been installed on the Green as a number of residents like to exercise their dogs on the lush green.

ELSTOW VILLAGE SIGN

It seems that a village sign for Elstow was first designed around 1920 as, in a book by Charles G. Harpur entitled "The Bunyan Country", the title page has a sketch of a sign named "Elstow". The following passage is taken from the book "In the craze for 'Village Signs' resulting from a suggestion by Prince Albert, Duke of York, at the Royal Academy banquet in 1920, many designs were exhibited, among them one for a double-sided sign for Elstow. This, resembling in shape a typical village inn-sign on a post showed Christian, in The Pilgrim's Progress, carrying his burden and was crested with a device portraying the fight between Christian and Apollyon. This remains only a design for it never was put into execution".

Mr Alan Chapman, a long standing resident of Elstow, was chairman of the Elstow Vanity Fayre 1988 Committee which was an off shoot from the Bunyan Festival 1988 Committee (the venture promoted by the Bedfordshire County Council when Elstow held the Vanity Fayre in July 1988). In his words by way of introduction at the official opening Mr Chapman found himself extemporising about how a stranger could walk from one end of the village to the other without being reminded that John Bunyan had lived there. He recalls how quite unexpectedly a vision of a village sign flashed across his mind and he knew he had a mission to erect a sign. He then remembered about a book he had read years earlier showing the Elstow sign. Mr Chapman decided to design a sign at an estimated cost of £2,500. The County Council had loaned money to those participating in the Bunyan Festival venture and the return of the unused money amounted to £2,300. Suggestions were invited as to its expenditure. Mr Chapman, sensing his vision of a village sign for Elstow might be possible, suggested such a project and it was agreed in view of the village's connection with John Bunyan. Following a public meeting the Elstow Parish Council agreed to meet the £250 shortfall.

The sign, which is in colour, was painted by the artist Graham Jones and depicts Christian carrying his burden, and a representation of Vanity Fayre on the Green on the other side. As part of all village signs there are bat wings below the sign. The sign stands on a brick plinth built by local builder Mr Michael Hurley, Mr Chapman acted as labourer. Watling and Dowling of Bedford were responsible for the woodwork, the siting and position of the sign was agreed by the County Council and British Telecom kindly assisted with the erection. The sign was unveiled by the Mayor of Bedford, Councillor Sylvia Gillard at an official ceremony in December 1989. The sign was repainted in 1997 by Wendy Norris.

Chapter 3

THE MOOT HALL

On the north side of the Green stands the timber framed building of the Moot Hall, which dates back to about 1500. Originally the timber frame was filled with wattle-and-daub. The curved tension braces join the upright posts to the horizontal plates and are halved into fairly wide spaced studs. It shows what a simple and logical work of structural engineering medieval carpenters produced. It was known as the Market House and has also been called the Green House. It is now a museum of 17th century life and traditions associated with the life of John Bunyan who is reputed to have preached in the Moot Hall.

The Moot Hall was probably built to house the stalls and equipment from the fairs held on the Green and as a Manor Court to hear and settle trading disputes and mete out local justice; it was also used for village purposes and nonconformists worship.

The building had four bays with six small shops, each with a separate door and single light window; the six doors can still be seen. One bay had a separate room with a rope staircase to the upper floor which is the long hall of today. Later a fifth bay, with a staircase, was added which had chimneys and fireplaces on both floors, so may have been used as a cottage. Until about 1873 the upper floor was used as a place of worship and during the week as a National School and Night School. The front of the lower floor was used by the Whitbread Estate for the storage of ladders etc.

About half a century ago the Moot Hall required extensive restoration and renovation so Major Simon Whitbread gave, by Deed of Gift, the building which had been owned by the Whitbreads for about one hundred and fifty years, to the Bedfordshire County Council so that the necessary repairs could be carried out in the Festival of Britain Year 1951.

It was the hope of the Festival of Britain Council that while the summer of 1951 would be a season of festivity and enjoyment, it would also be something more such as taking the opportunity to complete projects of lasting value to the

Moot Hall   *Photo by C. Marotta*

Festival of Britain Sign

Mrs Sarah Bowler and Sir Thomas Lipton outside the Moot Hall

34

community thereby leaving the nation and each locality within it, better off at the end of 1951 than when the year began. It was suggested that the year could serve as a spur to bring forward some scheme, or combine a series of activities and give them collective significance so making the year one in which something additional was achieved by the people of Britain. The objects of Bedfordshire County Council fell within the general principles and the paramount object had to be connected with the Christian religion. The County Council felt that Elstow Moot Hall was a worthy object and it would perpetuate the memory of perhaps the County's greatest son and world figure as a Christian preacher and author of The Pilgrim's Progress.

In the Official Book of the Festival of Britain 1951 it is stated "that buildings of historical importance or architectural beauty have been restored, among them the Guildhall at King's Lynn, the walls of Lewes Castle and the Moot Hall at John Bunyan's birthplace Elstow".

The Bedfordshire County Council erected village signs on approaches to villages showing the name of the village, the County Arms and the Festival of Britain emblem. The Elstow sign however stands on the High Street a few hundred yards from The Swan Public House.

The medieval roof of the Moot Hall was found to be largely intact but much work was needed on the ground and upper floors. Some of the timber was badly decayed and oak from Essex was used in the restoration. The Moot Hall re-opened on 31st May 1951. There was a service in the Church before the opening by Sir Thomas Keens, Chairman of Bedfordshire County Council.

The Moot Hall once had a custodian who was ninety years old and so fit and active that at the turn of the century (1900), she was asked to play a part in the advertising of a well known beverage. Mrs Sarah Bowler was the grandmother of a present resident of Elstow who has lived in the village all her life. It is not known exactly how Sir Thomas Lipton heard of Mrs Bowler but no doubt he was acquainted with the Whitbreads who employed her as custodian. It is understood that part of the advertisement showed Sir Thomas Lipton outside the Moot Hall presenting Mrs Bowler with a large box of Lipton's tea.

The present custodians are employed by the Bedfordshire County Council who undertake the care of the Moot Hall, which is open to the public from April to the end of September on Sunday, Tuesday to Thursday and Bank Holidays from 2.00 p.m. to 4.00 p.m. It is closed Monday, Friday and Saturday.

There is a nominal entrance fee of £1 for adults and 50p for Senior Citizens and children and there is a small car park.

During excavations of Elstow Abbey Church between 1965 and 1970 a late 8th century Saxon Cross shaft was found and this is on show in the Moot Hall.

For over forty years the Elstow Moot Hall Flower Group have provided floral displays in the Moot Hall during the summer months. Concerts of Period Music have been held in the long hall over the years and Harry Secombe recorded one of his "Highway" radio programmes from the Moot Hall. Elstow Lower School recorded one of their morning assemblies from the upper floor for radio too. Terry Waite has visited the Moot Hall, once in 1992 after his hostage experiences and again informally in 1994 to record an item for the radio programme "Going Places" which is about celebrities re-visiting places they have enjoyed visiting before.

The number of visitors to the Moot Hall seems to have declined in recent years; maybe with all the attractions nowadays a visit to an old historical building sounds boring, and costly. Of course all kinds of places can now be "visited" from the comfort of an armchair, but sometimes, a visit, in person, to a Moot Hall, an Ancestral Home or even a Watermill, can be quite informative and it is often interesting to see how our forebears lived in bygone days.

Chapter 4

THE SCHOOL

Elstow School, now known as Elstow Lower School, stands at the northern end of the High Street. It is believed that the Whitbreads gave the land for the school which was opened in September 1874 though construction presumably commenced in 1873 as a brick near the bottom of the front wall bears that date. The School used to cover the villages of Elstow, Wilstead, Haynes, Clophill, Cople and Cardington and had pupils from the age of 5 to 15.

The original school building with the attached head teacher's house, where the early headmasters and headmistresses lived, and which is now inhabited by the school caretaker cost £1,163. The building consisted of three classrooms and a cloakroom and constituted the main teaching area. In 1930 the middle and rear blocks were built, the former to cater for the increasing number of pupils and the rear block to provide suitable facilities for the teaching of science, woodwork and domestic science. The toilets were outside, a row in the girls' playground and a row in the boys' playground.

In 1958 the Abbey School on Mowbray Road opened for age eleven plus pupils. Elstow School then became a Junior School catering for children of 5 to 11 years. In the 1970s Bedfordshire County Council decided to adopt the 3-tier system. As a result, former Junior Schools were to be re-named Lower Schools, catering for children aged 5 to 9; former Secondary Modern Schools would become Middle Schools, with children aged 9+ to 12+ and schools with children aged 13 to 16 (18) would be named Upper Schools. Thus in 1976 Elstow School pupils had to transfer to the Middle School in the September following their ninth birthday. Today the catchment area is Elstow and part of Mile Road and the school has pupils from the age of 4+ to 9 years old.

In the early years the scholars' attendance at the school was not always good as many children stayed away at certain times to assist with haymaking, potato picking or other seasonal employment. Many girls were kept away to do lace making in order to earn a few pence towards the support of the family.

Illness, of course, was another and more legitimate reason and especially in 1887 when scarlet fever broke out in the village and three children from the infant's class died. The headmaster's daughter had died the year previously from suspected whooping cough. Around the same time there were outbreaks of typhoid, diphtheria and chicken pox in neighbouring villages. The children were allowed a day off from school for the Fairs held in the village in May and November and a half day, or early finish, for the May Festival on the Green.

After the Abbey School opened, the Elstow Craft Centre for Adult Education, sponsored by the County Education Committee, opened in the rear blocks of the school in 1967. The building was fully equipped for upholstery and furnishing crafts, dressmaking and cookery, and thus enabled housewives, and other people, who were unable to attend evening classes to learn various crafts and skills during the day. Patchwork, embroidery, soft toys, painting and millinery were also included over the years. The Craft Centre moved to a new venue in the mid-nineties and the building now houses a small computer room, a kitchen to prepare school meals and a dining room.

On top of the original school building is a small bell tower, which used to hold a bell which was rung for the start of the school day. It is not known for certain whether the present clock was actually given by Mr Wadsworth, a previous headmaster, though it was unveiled by Mrs Wadsworth in July 1964 to commemorate "The end of the war and happy May days held on Elstow Green". An inscription round the clock shows "Passing Rapidly Use Hours Wisely Happily".

The trees on the perimeter of the school grounds were planted by the pupils in 1931. The school still has two playgrounds and a playing field.

It is recorded that the first headmaster's salary was £75 a year. Over the years Elstow School has had some long serving staff. Mr James was headmaster from 1883 to 1921 and Mr Wadsworth, who was known as one of the characters of Bedfordshire education in his day, was headmaster from 1921 to 1949. He had a reputation of being very strict, and seems to have been well ahead of time in some aspects of education - school meals featured in the school long before they were made universal and experiments in agricultural education gained him more than local repute. Opposite the school was an allotment site owned by the school where Mr Wadsworth taught pupils how to cultivate the ground and grow crops. Another of Mr Wadsworth's achievements was the revival of the May Festival. He also had an Armstrong

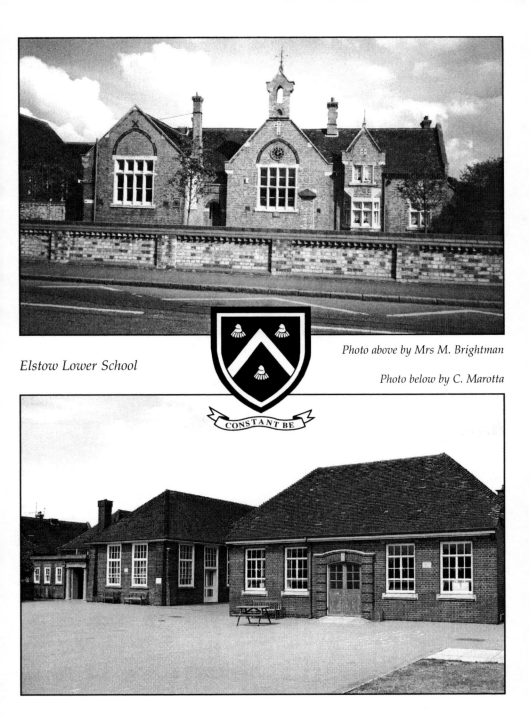

Elstow Lower School

Photo above by Mrs M. Brightman

Photo below by C. Marotta

CONSTANT BE

Elstow Lower School   *Photos by C. Marotta*

The Trees at Elstow Lower School (see page 38)

Sidley car which he kept in the garage at the side of the school house. A resident who still lives in the village and attended the school, clearly remembers the registration number as TN9 and how he, along with some other boys, had the job of cleaning the car every so often during the war years.

Mr Smith who was headmaster for eleven years was succeeded, in September 1965, by Mrs Blundell who had previously been headmistress at Cardington. When she retired in 1984, after nineteen years at Elstow, she was one of the longest serving head teachers in Bedfordshire, having been a headmistress for twenty-eight years. Mrs Blundell liked Elstow so much that when she retired she decided to remain in the village and is now one of the senior residents.

During Mrs Blundell's headship the school entered the Bedfordshire Music Festival for the first time in 1966 and was thrilled when the choir came first in the Small School Choir class and took part in the Final concert. Another good year was 1980 when the school came top in the Mixed Choir 19 and Under class and again first in the Small School Choir section. Over the years the school's success in the Music Festival has continued and in 1999 again came first in the Small School Choir class, and took part in the launch of the Children's University.

In 1966 the first Sports Day for many years was held on the school playing field. About this time there was an Education Authority scheme to provide certain schools with a learner swimming pool. The school had to be responsible for a share of the cost. Mrs Blundell founded a thriving Parent Teacher Association whose first task was to raise the required sum for a pool of their own. Once this was installed they continued their support and soon raised more cash to provide heating for the pool. The outdoor swimming pool was opened in September 1967 by Jeanette Stewart-Wood, the then World Water Ski Champion. As well as teaching all pupils to swim the school held Swimming Sports days. In October 1970 a Swimming Gala for Primary Schools, sponsored by Coca Cola Western Brothers Ltd., and in conjunction with the Bedford and District Schools' Swimming Association, was held at the Robinson Pool. This was the first of what became an annual event and in the first year Elstow School won the Small Schools' Trophy. Unfortunately, it was felt necessary to demolish the school swimming pool in the 1990s in case vandalism occurred in out of school hours. For a while pupils went by a hired bus to the Kempston Swimming Pool but this became too costly and too time consuming, so Elstow

School pupils now have to wait for swimming classes until they join the Middle School or go privately with their parents to the swimming pools in and around Bedford.

After a three year wait, the School's Parent Teacher Association were able to have a stall on the Bedford Saturday market in December 1974. Nearly £100 was raised from the sale of cakes, toys and novelty gifts towards staging for the school. Money continues to be raised for the school by various activities, a fairly new venture is the annual Governors' Fun Run.

The school's centenary was in 1974 and as part of the celebrations a play written by Mrs Blundell entitled "Welcome Back" was performed by pupils and members of the staff. The play involved pupils of 1874 meeting pupils of 1974 to show comparison in their way of school life with the various changes and modern methods regarding arithmetic, reading and drill (PE today). After the play other pupils took part in a pantomime of Red Riding Hood. The final event of the centenary year was a service of lessons and carols in the Church.

Milk used to be provided for pupils at break time but this ceased countrywide many years ago and only pupils in the 4+ units and those with a medical condition are now allowed milk.

In 1966 the school adopted the motto "Constant Be" which, of course, is taken from John Bunyan's famous hymn. At the same time a school badge was introduced. This was light blue on a navy background and consisted of three escallops from the Bedfordshire Arms and a chevron. An escallop is a common badge of pilgrims and a chevron denotes rank, in this case it symbolises younger members of the family. The badge was designed by a group of Elstow School pupils and is intended to mean "we are children of Bedfordshire on a pilgrimage".

Summer Fetes, admission to which twenty-five years ago was two and a half pence (2½d) and included a lucky number programme; various outings, though of course not so venturous as in 1972 when some of the senior scholars visited Paris for four days, and Sports Days, still continue to take place as they have done over the years and, of course, the May Festival now known as the Midsummer Festival. There are no Swimming Sports now nor an annual Prize Giving, though achievement awards are given weekly. Whereas years ago there used to be a Nativity Play performed by the younger pupils and a pantomime by the older ones, there is now a Christmas entertainment by the pupils, to which the old folk at Bunyan's Mead are invited, and the school has a

Christmas service in the Church.

Elstow School started an Out of School Club in 1994 which enabled children whose parents were not able to be at home at the usual school finishing time, to stay at school for up to an extra couple of hours until a parent could collect them. However, due to lack of funds the Club had to close about three years later.

In June 1999, as part of National Child Safety Week, the Bedfordshire and Luton Fire and Rescue Service launched a School Safety Education Programme and Elstow School was chosen to receive the first presentation. The pupils learned the basics of fire safety and what to do in an emergency as well as seeing the fire fighting equipment used by the Fire Service.

At the present time the Elstow Lower School has eight teachers and 206 pupils. The headmistress is Mrs Watson who has been at the school for two years.

A vehicular access to the school is on the other side of the Bunyan Meeting Chapel. As a sign of the times the school gates have to be closed during teaching time for security reasons. Like many schools countrywide Elstow School is used as a Polling Station for Parliamentary and Council elections.

While todays pupils face a more ambitious programme than in the past, it remains to be seen how much better their education will serve them, as they follow in the path of village life.

Unfortunately, some of the Elstow Lower School buildings are becoming outdated but whether necessary alterations will be carried out seems somewhat doubtful especially as a new school is apparently proposed near the Abbeyfields development - only time will tell.

MAY DAY FESTIVAL

The custom of celebrating May Day is very ancient. Although it is not known how far back May Day Festivals may have been held in Elstow, records show that there was a maypole in use in Elstow in 1875. The school log book records that children took part in festivities on the Green in that year and it is also recorded that in 1883 the children left school early in the afternoon and marched through the village to the Green to take an active part in the May Day Festival.

It was apparently the custom in the 1880s for Mrs Macan, who lived in Elstow Lodge, to provide a new dress and apron for the May Queen and new aprons for the Maids of Honour. After 1889 the May Day Festival lapsed until revived by Mr Wadsworth in 1925 when over one thousand people attended the event on the Green, some walking and cycling from Bedford and further afield. About two hundred pupils from the school took part and the late Charlie Prudden, an Elstow character, was one of the train bearers.

The Festival was not always held on May Day itself but generally in the early part of May. Although the Festival continued all through the Second World War it lapsed between 1968 and 1973. The May Festival has not always been held on the Green, but on the school playing field, as it is nowadays. However, when it did take place on the Green, the High Street had to be closed to traffic whilst the procession made its way from the school to the Green, quite a task for the police, especially as formerly the road was the main Bedford to London road, and in the years when there was a performance in the afternoon and again in the evening, though, of course, there would not have been so much traffic as in later years.

Between 1952 and 1962 the May Festival was featured on a BBC Television programme; a full page coloured photograph appeared in the National Geographic Magazine of America; the sleeve of a Country Dance gramophone record depicted Elstow children dancing on the Green. In 1962 Anglia Television covered the procession whilst the BBC Television covered the crowning ceremony and dancing. The well known artist Terence Cunes was commissioned in 1959 to paint a May Festival and chose Elstow. A reproduction of the picture used to hang in the school.

In past years, the May Queen was voted for in a secret ballot by the top class of the school. The coach was decorated by parents and teachers with thousands of paper flowers which were made by the parents. The coach was pulled by the older boys of the school, though on occasions four fathers have acted as "horses". The maypole, which had to be erected prior to the commencement of the proceedings, was carried at the head of the procession. Then followed the May Queen in her coach accompanied by the two train bearers. The coachman, who also acted as herald and announced the dances, was dressed in a coat of scarlet, white trousers, black boots and a black top hat. The Maids of Honour, two or three jesters who entertained the spectators during the afternoon with their various antics, and the remainder of the school

May Day Festival 1944

May Day Festival 2000

Photos by C. Marotta

children, carrying decorated branches of orange, yellow, white and red which made a colourful spectacle, followed the coach. The idea of carrying decorated branches probably came from Ancient Rome when the young people would show their joy that Spring had arrived by dancing and singing in the fields in honour of Flora their Goddess of fruit and flowers. In later Christian times people got up at sunrise to collect greenery and blossom and having chosen a King and Queen from their village to crown and honour, they processed through the streets.

Elstow School's May Festival, arrived on the Green or school field, as the case may be, and the May Queen, escorted by the Maids of Honour and preceded by the crown bearer carrying the crown on a pink cushion, made her way to the throne which was on a dais, where she was crowned by the previous year's May Queen. After being crowned, the May Queen would give a short speech of welcome to all present, request that the "messengers of peace", some white pigeons, be released and that the maypole and country dancing commence. For several years Mr Wagstaff, who still lives in the village, kept pigeons and these were used as the "messengers of peace". When there were two performances in the day, he had to have two lots of pigeons in case they did not all return to their loft in time for the second performance. In the time of Queen Elizabeth I, the custom of dancing round a garlanded pole was well established. Children of early schools used to join in the traditional activity on village greens each Maytime.

A collection was usually made for charity, money being collected on a blanket. After the activities the children returned to the school for well earned refreshments.

After a break of seven years, the May Festival was held again in 1974 as part of the school's centenary celebrations. It was held on the school's playing field and all 140 pupils took part. The 48th May Festival was held in 1978, this was as part of the tercentenary celebrations of the publication of The Pilgrim's Progress. For the first time in eleven years the Festival was held on the Green and it is recorded that three thousand people attended the event, the biggest crowd for many years. The headmistress renamed the familiar country and maypole dances with names relevant to the occasion, such as Tipcat Polka, Vanity Fayre and Pilgrim's Progress.

In both 1977 and 1978 the school took part in the Bedford Regatta by having a float in the road procession which bore the decorated coach with the

May Queen and her retinue and in the latter year even gave a performance by the river of their maypole dancing.

The May Queen of 1944 and some other pupils who took part in the May Festivals many years ago still live in the village. The May Festivals used to be a popular village attraction and drew large crowds.

Although the event still takes place in the school grounds before parents and invited audience, it is generally held in June because school assessments have to be undertaken in May. Nowadays it is a Summer Queen but she is still elected by the top class and the previous year's Queen performs the crowning ceremony. The dances include both traditional and modern with line dancing and ethnic dances.

It is good that the tradition is still kept up here in Elstow even if not on such a grand scale, but with the present school's curriculum, and all the modern technology, fitting in old customs can be quite difficult and time consuming.

It would be nice though to think of the ceremony returning to the Green, as in the past years, educational considerations permitting.

Chapter 5

THE HIGH STREET

Long ago the High Street, then known as "Village Street", was part of the main London, Carlisle, Inverness A6 road. As far back as 1930 a bypass for Elstow was suggested but not until 1974 was the matter proposed again. Eventually the bypass materialised and was opened on 15th November 1982. The bypass ran south from the junction of Ampthill Road and West End to join the A6 at the southern end of the village.

The High Street runs from Mile Road to the bridge which crosses the Elstow Brook where the road name changes to Wilstead Road. It is hard to believe that only a decade ago part of the High Street ran past allotments, a social club and a children's playground, although centuries ago, along with John Bunyan's cottage, there were other cottages on the roadside. Following the development of Progress Way and the Hillersden estate in 1991/92 the High Street was closed to vehicular traffic at the Mile Road end for safety reasons. The children's playground was moved nearer to the pedestrian railway bridge to Ampthill Road; meanwhile Progress Way, the Hillersden development along with Wigram Close and the nine new cottage homes occupy the site of the allotments and social club. Wigram Close, which was named after a well known Elstow family, and the cottage homes which bear names such as Damsel Cottage and Candlewick Cottage, were built in 1993/94.

There were some allotments on the east side of the High Street off Mile Road but these are now closed and the land awaits some kind of re-development.

Although John Bunyan was born at Harrowden just across the fields from the main village of Elstow (a stone in the fields marks the site of his birth place), he was baptised in the Abbey Church at Elstow on 13th November 1628 at the same font which is used in the Church today. John Bunyan, like his father, was originally a brazier and tinker. After his marriage he moved into the village of Elstow and lived in a cottage on the High Street which was nearly opposite the present school. He attended services at the Church for many years and was also a bell ringer. John Bunyan moved into Bedford in 1655. He died in London in 1688 having caught a chill whilst riding in the rain to London and was buried in Bunhill Fields, off the City Road. A large altar tomb showing the reclining figure of John Bunyan sculptured in stone marks the spot. The tomb has been restored in recent years.

In later years John Bunyan's cottage became a hardware shop and then a sweet shop which was run by a Miss Fox. It was repaired in 1944 after a lorry ran into it causing a fatal accident. It remained inhabited for at least a further 20 years although it seemed to be a target for the continuous heavy traffic which travelled along the High Street. Eventually it was decided that the cottage should be demolished and Thursday 19th September 1968 was a sad day for the village when by the evening of that day John Bunyan's cottage was no more. A sign, made by Mr Peter Pestell, was placed outside the present St. Helena Restaurant to mark the approximate site where the cottage had stood. However, with the new development of the High Street the sign was removed and placed, for safety, in the grounds of the St. Helena. This was only visible to the patrons of the restaurant, so a new stone plaque, designed by Mr Alan Chapman, was kindly given by the owner of the St. Helena Restaurant, Mr Raffaele Marotta, and placed on the wall outside by the main entrance so that all visitors to Elstow can see whereabouts the cottage used to stand.

The St. Helena Restaurant is a 16th century house with Victorian additions. It used to be a residential house with a small holding and during the last war Mrs Humphries, the lady of the house, along with her daughter and their maid, provided food such as pies and sausage rolls to the needy of the village. The house was also used as a First Aid and A.R.P. post. It has been a country house restaurant of elegance and distinction since the early 1980s and attracts the more affluent clientele. Lunches are served from Tuesday to Friday and Dinners from Tuesday to Saturday evenings. It is rumoured that centuries ago there may have been a tunnel from the house to the Church and a lady with a white dog is reputed to haunt the upstairs of the house from time to time.

The four remaining cottages on this part of the High Street date from around the 17th century. One of the cottages has a thatched roof and is one of only three thatched cottages left in the village. This cottage is a listed building, as are a number of residences in the village. The interior has the original wooden beams and used to be two cottages, of one room up and one room

John Bunyan's Cottage

The Old High Street

The St. Helena Restaurant   *Photos by C. Marotta*

The Grounds of St. Helena Restaurant (see page 50)

down. The present occupier, whose in-laws were the first couple to be married in the Elstow Bunyan Meeting Chapel, has lived in the cottage for over forty years following her marriage to Peter Pestell the son of a local farmer (Mr H. W. Pestell) who had an arable and dairy farm and small holding in the village. Mrs Pestell also lived in Bunyan's cottage for about four years from 1954. Grandmother Lavina, who lived next door to the post office, did the laundry for some people in the village before 1880 and used to hang the washing across the Green. The Lace School was held in one of these cottages.

The Bunyan Meeting Chapel stands on the High Street adjacent to the school. The Congregational Nonconformists met in the Green House (Moot Hall) for worship from 1812 until the Bunyan Meeting Chapel was built in 1910. The land for the building was given by Mr Whitbread and many donations were received towards the cost of the Chapel. Mr E. P. Rose who owned the departmental store in Bedford, now owned by Debenhams, kindly doubled the amount of the donations and also donated a stained glass window in memory of his wife.

The Chapel opened on 27th October 1910 and for the fifty years celebration in 1960 a special service was held in the building which was attended by former Bunyan Meeting Ministers.

In the Chapel is a beautiful stained glass window in three tiers depicting The Pilgrim's Progress. There are also two plaques, one dedicated to Mr Poynter who was a Deacon of the Chapel and the other to William Arthur Cirket who was a founder member of the Bunyan Meeting Chapel. Mr Cirket organised all kinds of activities for fund raising including a large sale of work towards the cost of a new organ in 1892, a harmonium had been used in the Moot Hall up to that time. Mr Cirket was the first organist at the Bunyan Meeting Chapel and played for many years, being followed by his son William in 1921, grandson Alan also played from the 1950s to 1995. Mr W. A. Cirket started a Coal Club in the 1890s and also a Clothing Club which was still in existence in the 1960s. The money was paid back annually with interest just before Easter and the clothing could be purchased at Braggins, which was a large store in Bedford. The Cirkets were a well known family and six generations lived in the village of Elstow for almost two hundred years. Alan was at one time secretary to the Elstow Cricket Club, nowadays he gives talks and slide shows to various clubs and organisations in and around Bedford, concerning old Bedford, Elstow, John Bunyan and other historical topics on which he is a mine of information.

Nothing has changed much over the years in the Elstow Bunyan Meeting Chapel which is, of course, linked to the Bunyan Meeting in Mill Street, Bedford. Services are held regularly on a Sunday though attendance is not as good as in years gone by. On Remembrance Sunday, after the services in the Church and the Chapel, the Vicar of the Abbey Church and the Minister of the Chapel, together with members of both congregations, join in a short service of remembrance and the laying of wreaths at the War Memorial.

The War Memorial stands in the front grounds of the Elstow Lower School. It cost £150 and was sponsored by public subscription and erected by the parishioners of Elstow. It is a truncated nine foot high obelisk of Cornish grey granite on a sandstone plinth and was unveiled in November 1919 by Mr Samuel Howard Whitbread, the then Lord Lieutenant of Bedfordshire. The school flag was at half mast and the ceremony was attended by pupils from the school and village residents. Mr Poynter, the Chairman of the Committee responsible for the arrangements, read the appointed memorial prayer and following the unveiling, a wreath of laurels and floral tributes were laid by relatives of those who had died. The inscription on the War Memorial reads:-

> "In grateful memory of these men of Elstow who gave
> their lives to preserve our liberties in the Great War
> 1914-1918".

There are eleven names from the Great War and three from the Second World War engraved thereon, in alphabetical order.

The War Memorial is recorded in the National Inventory of War Memorials held by the Imperial War Museum, as is one in the Elstow Bunyan Meeting Chapel which also records the names of ten men who attended the Chapel who were killed in the Great War.

According to some records the Red Lion which stands at the junction of the High Street and West End could have been in business in 1600 although the date on the building shows 1789. It is one of the two remaining public houses in Elstow; there used to be five. The Red Lion, as well as being a public house, now has a Brewers Fayre Restaurant and exterior play area for children. At one time there were stables in the grounds which are now used by the Red Lion as store houses. Over the years the Red Lion has been enlarged and new exterior lighting has been installed.

The Elstow Bunyan Meeting Chapel (see page 53)   Photos by Mrs M. Brightman

War Memorial

Jetty (see page 61)

Red Lion Public House   *Photo by Mrs M. Brightman*

The High Street with Post Office on right   *Photo by C. Marotta*

Next to the Red Lion is a very old house, probably dating back to the 16th century which it is understood has always been pebbledashed. Simmons, the well known Elstow Florists now live in the house. Alongside the house is a brick building built in 1888 as a bakehouse. Tradition has it that the baker committed suicide by shooting himself. This building is now used by Simmons for the sale of plants, flowers and vegetables and where they make up their bouquets, wreaths and floral arrangements. It is believed that a cottage stood where the entrance to the florists is and that the site was a market garden, today it is the nursery for the fresh flowers and vegetables.

On the opposite side of the High Street is the Post Office which has been on the same site since 1700 and can be seen on old photographs of Elstow. At one time the postmaster was also the village postman and three generations of the Southam family ran the Post Office for many years. The Post Office part has been extended and now sells groceries and cards etc.

The house next to the Post Office, known as Pilgrim House was built in 1806. It has been extensively renovated and the garden fence replaced by a brick wall during the last decade.

The front of the cottage on the corner of Church End is known to date from 1300 whilst the rest of the cottage is around the 17th century. The cottage has a crown post roof which is quite rare. It is likely that Abbotts lived in the cottage centuries ago. The cottage is known as Green Corner and it would have been on the Green before the Moot Hall car park was constructed. A well, which is recorded as being on the Green and into which a boy attending the Lace School threw his pillow after a scolding, is believed to be the one found in the cottage garden. In the Deeds of the cottage the owners are allowed to have one ox and two goats tethered on the Green. It was one of only three privately owned cottages in the village and before the present owners moved in some years ago, it used to be the Village Store owned by the Cave family. The entrance to the shop was down a steep step from the High Street. The shop sold food as well as household items; paraffin could also be purchased, this was stored in a tank outside. It was seldom that an item required was not available.

The Swan is the other public house and dates back to at least 1799. There used to be stables, later used as garages, on the Church End side of the present car park. For many years it was run by two generations of the same family. It is a Greene King property and here again has undergone many alterations over the years. Food is available and served throughout most of the day. There is a cosy lounge bar area with an open fire for chilly days, or a restaurant for 22 diners. Many dishes are homemade and can be accompanied by a selection of "Real Ales". The Swan has a good car park and a walled garden.

Next to The Swan is a late medieval, maybe 1400, cottage where a well known dairy farming family lived. The sole survivor, Charlie Prudden, died in 1996 and the cottage has undergone complete restoration. Whilst the contractors were removing the rendering from the outside walls of the cottage a doorway was discovered with some well preserved wooden carving above it.

It was a regular occurrence for cows to be herded along the High Street to the various fields for grazing. No doubt quite a traffic stopper but a real village scene. Four fields were used, one where Lynn Close now is, one behind Bunyan's Mead, another at the back of the houses on West End and the other on Church End, where there was also an orchard. At times the Pruddens were granted permission to graze their cows on the Green, and an evacuee from London who was billeted in Elstow and stayed on after the war, used to work at the farm and remembers controlling the cows on the Green when this was allowed. Charlie Prudden used to do a milk round with a horse and cart and although some of the milk was in bottles, the majority was sold from the churn and ladled into jugs on the doorstep - happy days!

Charlie Prudden was quite a character in the village. He knew everything that went on in Elstow but he also knew a great deal about the history of the village - it is a pity that he had passed on before this book was contemplated.

BUNYAN'S MEAD

The most striking cottages in Elstow are the black and white timbered ones on the High Street, though their address is now Bunyan's Mead.

Originally the cottages, thought to date from around the Jacobean period or even earlier, were black and white as today, but at some time in their existence were pebbledashed. In the 1970s the Whitbread estate sold the cottages to the Bedford Borough Council for one pound. The Council restored them to the original black and white, at the same time converting them into flats and maisonettes for the elderly with a daytime centre and resident warden flat with built in alarm system.

The Florist (see page 57)   *Photos by Mrs M. Brightman*

Charlie Prudden's House and The Swan Public House

Bunyan's Mead

Photos by Mrs M. Brightman

Thorogood's Yard (see page 62)

The cottages had big gardens and the present bungalows were built on them. The bungalows and cottage-cum-flats were opened in October 1977 during the Jubilee Year of Queen Elizabeth II.

One garden in particular grew herbs, vegetables and had fruit trees and when the bungalows were built, one resident had the tenancy of one which was actually built in her family's garden, so still has one of the fruit trees planted by her father.

There is an archway leading through to the bungalows from the High Street which is known as The Jetty. At one time it was also called Marble Arch. The reason for these names is not known, but the ancient hostelry which has been made into two upstairs flats and houses the daytime centre and an office on the ground floor, used to be a coaching inn, known as the White Lion and no doubt the horse drawn coaches pulled up by The Jetty and travellers stayed at the inn.

Whilst work was being carried out on the cottages it was discovered that the main living room of the upstairs flat, which was for the resident warden, was the first floor of a once free standing house. The room had probably been panelled as remains of panelling were found around the fireplace. The adjoining flat was probably a dormitory for the White Lion and three original window openings survived in the flat, two were already there and the other was discovered during the restoration work. The day centre, otherwise known as the residents communal sitting room, and the adjoining small room used as an office, were restored as far as possible to their original condition of around the 17th century. The small room which is panelled has 18th century cupboards either side of the fireplace. The communal sitting room is also panelled with some of the original panelling over the fireplace. The staircase was restored to its original well and carved and turned to the original designs. Two Coats of Arms were found over the fireplaces in the two rooms. One being that of William Parker, whose wife was sister of one of the Gunpowder Plot conspirators. Not much is known about the other apart from the fact that it is continental, possibly German work. Both Coats of Arms were encrusted with paint when found but after protracted cleaning the delicacy of the designs became apparent. Why the Coats of Arms became fixed in the old building is not known but it is thought that some were put in inns under regular patronage of the nobility as a form of "by appointment" reservation of accommodation, but then again they may have arrived out of the blue!

The cottages are frequently photographed by visitors to the village and sketched and painted by visiting artists.

The bungalows and flats are warden controlled and most are owned by the Bedfordshire Pilgrim Housing Association. The residents of Bunyan's Mead meet in the communal sitting room for various activities and the Vicar of the Abbey Church celebrates Holy Communion at the Centre once a month.

In addition to the bungalows at Bunyan's Mead there are some houses and a car park. The space between the old cottages, by the bus stop, was known as Thorogood's Yard and there was a barn where a cobbler worked. The last detached house, before the bridge crosses the Elstow brook, bears the date 1796 and S.W. At one time this was a blacksmiths and forge and no doubt kept busy with the horse drawn carriages which travelled through the village. Well over half a century ago, it became the local garage with three petrol pumps and also did vehicle repairs. Before becoming a private residence it was a warehouse for Schweppes.

A right of way alongside the brook used to cross moors to the Gostwick Road shops. The shops can still be reached by the pathway as can Pilgrims Way and the Abbey School.

Chapter 6

WEST END

West End used to be known as "The Lane" and until the construction of the Elstow Bypass in 1982 used to run straight from the junction of the High Street, westwards towards Ampthill Road. At that time the four old cottages and the twelve terraced houses at the top end of West End were on the main part of the road, but to accommodate the Cowbridge roundabout a service road, still known as West End, was made thus leaving the houses back from the main road. The original part of West End joins Progress Way at the roundabout which was constructed in 1997 as a safety measure for the entrance road to the Abbeyfields development.

The four old cottages with the leaded light windows, on the service road, date from 1818 and have recently been renovated. One of the houses used to have an aviary and sold birds and bird seed etc. The houses in St. Mary's Close were built about 1996 on some of the back gardens of the terraced houses which date from around 1900. The name of St. Mary's Close was suggested to the developer by the Elstow Parish Council. Right at the end of the service road, more or less hidden from view, are two houses one of which, at one time, had a wood yard and supplied bundles of wood, some of which were sold at the village post office.

On the other part of West End (High Street end) are nine old terraced houses and two detached houses, some bear the date 1903 and some 1908 but all have S.W. on them, showing that they belonged to the Whitbread estate. The terraced houses are in groups of three, so from the High Street there is one group then the detached houses before the other two groups of three. All these houses have chimney stacks with reconstituted stone caps and have verandah style roofs between gable ends. They have big front gardens with vehicle access to most along a road off West End, though the very end house has an entrance from the High Street. The houses had their chimney pots replaced around 1996/97 but they were, of course, kept to the original style. Nowadays most newly built houses do not have chimney pots (However does Santa Claus get in?). The two houses nearest the roundabout are about three years old and the other was built in 1999.

Between the old detached houses was a narrow pathway which led from West End across the fields to the pedestrian bridge over the Bedford to Bletchley railway line to the Ampthill Road. Alexanders which is a bushy plant with umbels of yellow-green flowers has been growing along this pathway for hundreds of years. The plant which is a kind of vegetable and medicinal herb, with stems eaten like celery, can often be found under old hedges near ruins of abbeys. It is, therefore, quite likely that the footpath was part of the Abbey gardens and the nuns used the alexanders as a flavouring for the fish from the fishponds. As a note of interest, at the end of the pathway on Ampthill Road is a boundary marker dated 1934 showing Bedford to the north and Kempston to the south. The pathway still goes from West End to the railway bridge but passes through Wigram Close, across Progress Way and through the Hillersden development.

The path between the old houses was always becoming overgrown and muddy, despite in later years being maintained by the Borough Council. However in 1998 it was cleared, widened and resurfaced through the Parish Paths Partnership Scheme, since which it has been owned by the Parish Council. A dog waste bin was erected by the Borough Council.

Bedfordshire is part of the Parish Paths Partnership which is a national scheme initiated by the Countryside Commission whereby a grant is available from participating highway authorities to Parish Councils for a period of three years to enable them to improve the rights of way in their area. Many rights of way are in poor condition and part of the scheme is for paths to be upgraded and re-opened by undertaking vegetation clearance and by way marking. Elstow joined the scheme in 1997 and the new kissing gate and directional signs erected in late 1999 were obtained through the Parish Paths Partnership following liaison with local residents. The sculptor, Susannah Oliver designed both the kissing gate and the signs. The signs depict John Bunyan walking on the path towards the Abbey Church through the alexanders. It is hoped that the alexanders will continue to flourish in the area for years to come.

At one side of the entrance to the path was an old farm gate which led into the field where Wigram Close is situated. The space between the path and the boundary of the house became neglected over the years and was even used for

West End prior to becoming a service road

Hillesden Avenue (see page 67)   *Photos by C. Marotta*

Wigram Close (see page 49)

fly tipping. However, this strip of land has been cleared, fenced off and belongs to the house whose garden it once bordered.

The two cottages, next to the clapping gate on to the Green, are very old, around the 17th century. The six bungalows were built where some old cottages once stood and these belong to the Bedfordshire Pilgrim Housing Association.

A thatched barn stood on West End where corn was stored before being threshed. There was also a barn where potatoes were stored and a milking parlour which was used by Mr H. W. Pestell around 1920 and later by Charlie Prudden.

PROGRESS WAY AND HILLERSDEN ESTATE

Progress Way and the Hillersden Estate were built on the allotments and fields which were to the west of Mile Road.

In 1991 the developers asked Elstow Parish Council to suggest a name for the new road from Mile Road to the A6 Cowbridge roundabout prior to construction of the Hillersden development. The Parish Council decided to run a competition involving the pupils of the Elstow Lower School. Many names were submitted but the Parish Council liked Progress Way the best as it incorporated John Bunyan and the progress being made. The Parish Council awarded a £5 Gift Voucher to the pupil who suggested this name. The name was approved by the Borough Council as were the other names suggested by the Parish Council for the Hillersden development itself, which has about 180 properties. All the names have a connection with Elstow, John Bunyan or past well known residents, such as Hillersden Avenue after the Hillersden Manor House (due to an unfortunate oversight this road name was incorrectly spelt, the "r" being omitted); St. Helena Gardens after the Abbey Church; Tipcat Close - John Bunyan played tipcat on the Green; Prudden Close after an old farming family; Belfry Close - the Church Bell Tower and Little Townsend Close - family connections.

Chapter 7

THE PLAYING FIELD ASSOCIATION SPORTS AND SOCIAL CENTRE

The Elstow Playing Field Sports and Social Centre and the children's play area on Wilstead Road are rather unusual in that they are owned by the Elstow Playing Field Association which is a rare situation these days. Unfortunately some people are under the impression that the field is Council owned and that this gives them the right to abuse the facilities.

The field was originally owned by the Whitbread Estate but a tenant farmer allowed the cricket and football clubs to use the field free of charge. Both clubs, however, had to leave when the tenancy changed hands about forty years ago. Whilst waiting for a new playing field the cricket club played their fixtures at Bedford Park and the football club on a pitch in Moor Lane.

Following this slight upset a Playing Field Association Committee was formed with much help from some new residents, who were mainly ex-personnel of Cardington Camp, and who had moved into the newly built Lynn Close and Pear Tree View houses. About 1964 the Association was able to purchase eight acres of the original field. Three of the founder members still serve on the Committee.

When the playing field first came into being grass tennis courts stood where the car park is now but these had to be removed when the newly formed Tennis Club were unable to maintain them.

There used to be a football pitch at the far end of the present field. A hut, complete with a sunken bath, served as a changing room for the teams. This hut, although somewhat derelict, stands on the opposite side of the road in a garden alongside the Wilstead Road. It must have been quite a trek for the teams especially on a wet day! The hut was eventually sold to Mr Wagstaff for £15 and for some years after the war a notice was displayed on the wall above the bath which read:-

> "On the field you have played the game
> Regarding soap please do the same".

referring, of course, to the rationing of soap in those days.

It is understood that a track across the old playing field was used as a parade ground by a battalion of Scottish soldiers in the First World War.

Near where the car park is there used to be two very large holes presumably from which gravel had been extracted at some time for construction purposes elsewhere. Before these holes were filled in they made very good toboggan and motor bike slopes. Several residents remember the fun they had tobogganing and motor biking up and down these holes.

In the late 1920s a purpose built building, subscribed for by the villagers, was erected near where the telephone box at Bunyan's Mead stands. This was for the use of the whole community for various activities organised by the Playing Field Association and the Church. It was also used by the Scouts. Not long after the Second World War the famous entertainer, Wilfred Pickles, came to Elstow and recorded his "Have A Go" show in the building.

The hall was eventually pulled down to make way for the Bunyan's Mead development. The Playing Field Association then obtained an old wooden R.A.F. hut from Cardington. This served the community well for many years until the present Sports and Social Centre was built in 1988. The Centre comprises a large club room, kitchen, committee room, toilets and changing rooms. As well as being used for weekly bingo, short mat bowls and table tennis, the Centre can also be hired for Wedding receptions, meetings and exhibitions etc.

The Playing Field Association has four active sports clubs, as well as short mat bowls and four table tennis teams, there are two football teams and three cricket teams. All the clubs achieve much success.

Summer Fetes used to be popular but these ceased a few years ago; it seems that car boot sales, generally on the first Sunday of the month during the summer, and the occasional Race Night are a more profitable source of income nowadays. There used to be an Old Age Pensioners party near Christmas but this had to be discontinued due to lack of support. Like most villages, Elstow held Garden and Produce Shows with cups for the winners. These Shows used to be held in the School before the Sports and Social Centre was built as there was more space. Sadly these Shows became less popular and eventually ceased about two decades ago.

In 1991 the Bedfordshire Rural Community Council set a village challenge entitled "Celebrations". It was a competition where as many people who lived, or had lived, in a village could become involved in a project and show their particular talent.

Many villages took part, and after discussion, Elstow decided to organise a Craft Fair and Exhibition called "Made in Elstow". The response was terrific and 24th November saw the inside of the Sports and Social Centre transformed into a Lacemaker's Cottage, a Woodworker's Barn and Ye Olde Tea Shoppe with waitresses in Victorian costume. There were displays of painting and embroidery and the photographs of Elstow May Day Festivals were popular. The villagers who took part either exhibited or demonstrated their crafts with some also for sale. Later in the afternoon some of the exhibited crafts were included in a raffle along with a Bedfordshire Clanger; a Bedfordshire Clanger is made with suet crust pastry; it is an oblong shape rather like a long wide sausage roll. One end is filled with small pieces of bacon and onion, though meat and potato can be used, the other end is spread with jam or fruit filling. It is cooked by wrapping in greaseproof paper and pudding cloth and placed in boiling water and simmered for about two hours - a two course meal in one!

The Judges who visited during the morning appeared quite impressed with the way the crafts had been displayed and this proved correct when Elstow was finally declared the winner and presented with a cheque for £250 by Malcolm Singer from Three Counties Radio. The winners were also interviewed for a programme which was broadcast the following Sunday afternoon.

Most of the villages who entered the competition held Craft Fairs and the event was judged on various points, such as presentation, success of event. Three villages were awarded the third prize of £50 each and two villages were placed second receiving £100 each. Mrs Patey, who lives in the village and writes poems as a hobby, in the extract from her "Made in Elstow" poem sums up the day and talent in the village -

> "There was wooden toys, and so much more,
> I never knew there was so much talent in the village before,
> The Judges I thought were very wise,
> When they awarded 'Made in Elstow' with first prize".

In the 1999 Borough of Bedford Intervillage Games in which sixteen villages took part in various sporting activities with a trophy being awarded to the winners, Elstow entered the Short Mat Bowls competition and were runners up. Elstow also hosted the Table Tennis competition.

The Sports and Social Centre   *Photos by C. Marotta*

The Playground

Elstow Football Team 1960

Elstow Cricket Team, early fifties

Several years ago a glider landed unexpectedly in the playing field as did a hot air balloon on a similar occasion.

In late 1996 the committee room was recarpeted and new chairs and tables obtained with some money donated by the Parish Council. The car park was also resurfaced. About the same time, the children's play area had safety surfacing laid and all the equipment was renewed. The play area has swings, slides and a roundabout and caters for children up to the age of twelve.

Maintenance of the playing field, social centre and play area is all carried out by members of the Playing Field Committee. Unfortunately, like other places countrywide Elstow Sports and Social Centre is not exempt from vandalism. Damage at times can be quite severe and costly to repair incurring an increase in insurance. Dogs and the playing of golf are not allowed on the playing field.

An extension to the Sports and Social Centre is expected to be undertaken in the near future. Grants in the region of £42,000 from the Borough Council, Landfill Tax Credit Scheme and the Harrowden Planning Gain monies have been received towards the cost of this project.

Chapter 8

WILSTEAD ROAD

Travelling south through the village towards the A6 over the bridge which crosses Elstow Brook the road becomes Wilstead Road. The Elstow Brook, which is a minor tributary of the Great Ouse, rises from a spring line at the base of Lower Greensand Ridge southwest of Bedford and flows north eastwards, passing immediately south of Elstow Abbey towards Harrowden where it joins Medbury brook near Bumpy Lane at Old Harrowden. In 1993, prior to the construction of the Bedford Southern Bypass, remedial work along Elstow Brook was carried out by the Bedford and River Ivel Internal Drainage Board to reduce the risk of flooding southeast of Bedford. The Elstow Brook was quite probably the water source for the Abbey. There were also fishponds in the vicinity which would have provided the Abbey with fish for meals on a Friday. These were filled in many years ago by a local farmer.

The first dwelling on Wilstead Road is Elstow Lodge which used to be a large residential house but is now a privately run Home for the Handicapped. Elstow Lodge, as it is today, was built about 1926 although there had been a house, known as the Elstow Lodge, on the site for at least a century previously. It is thought that members of the Hillersden family lived in the original house at one time, as did the Wigram family. Turner Arthur Macan who was born on 9th June 1826 and died in 1889 and his wife Florence Louisa Jane Macan lived in Elstow Lodge towards the end of the 19th century. Mr Macan kept harriers from 1852 to 1864. Mrs Macan who was born on 19th September 1829 and died in Salisbury on 28th December 1919 was the lady who provided the dresses for the May Queens and was a School Governor and also a Magistrate. Both Turner and Florence are buried in Elstow Abbey Churchyard. The Macans were related to the Whitbreads viz Turner Macan's mother Harriett was first married to a General Macan and later became William Henry Whitbread's second wife, hence Turner Macan was the stepson of William Henry Whitbread. The Jefferson family lived in Elstow Lodge during the Great War.

The well known Graham family lived in the present Elstow Lodge for many years. Mr Graham was Clerk to the County Council. The Grahams had a herd of Jersey cows and a dairy where they made delicious butter. Mr Berwick, Mrs Roberts' father, (Mrs Roberts is an Elstow resident) used to work at Elstow Lodge and helped to make the butter. During part of the Graham's time at Elstow Lodge it was used as a residence by the Judge when the Assizes were in session in Bedford. It was a common sight, at that time, to see a big limousine carrying the Judge travelling along the High Street with a police escort on the way to and from the Court. Whilst the Judge was in residence Mrs Graham and family moved to other accommodation.

Shoots of game were controlled from Elstow Lodge and at one time a current resident of Elstow used to be a beater.

It is possible that there was a tunnel under the road from the Abbey to Elstow Lodge. There also used to be a path to the Church over a small bridge which crossed the brook in a field opposite Elstow Lodge; the brickwork of the bridge still stands today. In the last war there was a pill-box opposite the gateway of Elstow Lodge.

Since 1998 there has been a large housing development at the back of Elstow Lodge known as Abbeyfields, which has executive type houses as well as some social housing. The vehicle entrance to this development is off the new roundabout at the junction of West End and Progress Way on to a road which runs behind the Church and the Sports and Social Centre playing field and then adjacent to the Bedford Southern Bypass. A footpath has been constructed from Wilstead Road alongside Elstow Lodge to Abbeyfields. The roads in this development all bear the names of Abbeys, such as Melrose, Lilleshall, Kirkstall, Dorchester, Romsey, Titchfield and Whitby.

Along from Elstow Lodge is Holly Cottage which was built in John Bunyan's time around 1650. It was originally a four roomed cottage with a thatched roof and has always been privately owned. It is reputed that John Bunyan often called at the cottage as a visitor. At one time fruit and honey could be obtained from here, so no doubt, there were beehives as well as an orchard in the large garden. The cottage has been extended over the years but still has a big garden and the present owners graze sheep on the land. In the late 1950s there was a Riding School on land adjacent to the cottage at the back of Elstow Lodge but unfortunately this closed after three or four years.

The detached house next to Holly Cottage is well over one hundred years old and is a listed building. It used to be a bakery and the old ovens are still in part of the house. The baker used to deliver the bread by horse and cart. When the baker gave up, the next family to tenant the house kept cows which were grazed on two fields in the village and sold some of the milk in and around the village with the rest being sold wholesale.

The present tenants are Mr and Mrs F Wagstaff who have lived in the house for the last forty-five years. Mr Wagstaff kept threshing machines which were used to help the local farmers all the year round. He had three steam engines which drove the threshing machines. In the last war Mr Wagstaff had some Land Army girls working for him and they helped with the threshing. Mr Wagstaff himself, was an ARP warden during the war. The Wagstaffs are a long standing Elstow family; Mr Wagstaff (senior) used to live in Church End, his son Fred also lived in Church End when first married, and Fred's brother is still a resident in the village. Mr and Mrs Wagstaff can tell many tales about Elstow. This is the house where the old football hut is in the garden.

On the opposite side of the road is a 17th century detached house known as Acacia Cottage. This used to be two cottages, as was another detached house further up the road. Acacia Cottage has had several alterations and additions over the years.

Back across the road again is Village Farm House which, as the name suggests, was occupied for many years by farming families. Before the construction of the Bedford Southern Bypass could be undertaken archaeological investigations had to be carried out in various areas along the proposed route. Village Farm was known as the site of two ring-ditches probably the remains of neolithic or Bronze Age burial mounds. Parts of the ditches still survive in adjacent fields. The site could have been occupied during the Iron Age as there was evidence of timber structures and large pits probably dug for storage, while pottery of the Iron Age period was also discovered. There is talk that the dilapidated outbuildings may be made into residential dwellings but the future of the Village Farm House seems uncertain.

Like Village Farm House, the gamekeeper's cottage next door has an entrance at the side of the building instead of on Wilstead Road itself. There were a family of gamekeepers in the village by the name of Burr. Joe lived in the Gamekeeper's Cottage and bred pheasants and had kennels in the garden which housed the dogs, mostly spaniels, who took part in the Game Shoots. His brother Ernie lived on West End and controlled the beaters for the Shoots.

Constructing the bridge on Wilstead Road (see page 79)   *Photos by Mrs S. King*

Diversion on Wilstead Road

Works under the bridge   *Photos by Mrs S. King*

Bridge progressing

Joe took part in the "Have A Go" programme when Wilfred Pickles visited Elstow. A relative of the Burr family still lives in the village. Some Quaker graves are reputed to be at the back of the Gamekeeper's Cottage.

During the last decade a house and a bungalow have been built where a pair of old cottages once stood.

Past these residences is a detached house, which here again used to be two cottages. Over half a century ago this was the last building on this side of the road until Moss Lane. Following her retirement a distinguished headmistress of the Elstow Lower School lived in the house until in more recent years the bungalow next door was built.

Returning to the other side of Wilstead Road just up from the Sports and Social Centre is Lynn Farm House. The Prole family farmed both Lynn Farm and Village Farm which were two of the many farms in Elstow. As well as an arable farm Lynn Farm had pigs. One of the fields was known as Moss Close; this was where the houses on Pear Tree View now stand. Grandfather Prole built an extension to Lynn Farm House from bricks obtained from Old Warden. He was a churchwarden at the Elstow Abbey Church for forty years and his son, who was also a churchwarden, beat his father by two years. For many years, Miss Prole, who still lives in the house, was a bell ringer at the Church and in the late 1950s tolled the bells for funerals for the princely sum of two shillings and sixpence (2s.6d). The Prole family gave the present altar rails to the Church.

During the last war a German Prisoner of War lived at Lynn Farm and helped on the farm having been hired from the Prisoner of War Camp at Milton Ernest which was possibly the only Camp in Bedfordshire. Nowadays Lynn Farm House stands quite near to the bridge which crosses the Bedford Southern Bypass and it is understood that some bungalow development is contemplated for the derelict barns.

When the Bedford Southern Bypass was proposed, much to the alarm of the Elstow residents, it was routed to go through the village from east to west thus literally cutting the village in half. However, after much discussion with all concerned and as a compromise it was agreed to put the road under the Wilstead Road instead of over it. This, of course, caused more construction work, including the construction of a bridge, and as it was part of the flood plain, a pumping station had to be installed below the bridge so that the excess water could be continually pumped away. Unfortunately due to the route of the bypass a detached house which stood next to Lynn Farm House had to be demolished. It was originally an old wooden house which was later enlarged and rendered. The occupants, of course, received compensation, but it was a sad sight to see a good residence go under the diggers.

The construction of the Bedford Southern Bypass was undertaken by Wimpey-Amey (Joint Venture). Thorburn Colquhoun, consulting engineers, based in Bedford, prepared the scheme on behalf of the Highways Agency, an Executive Agency of the Department of Transport. Both the consulting engineers and contractors did their utmost to keep noise and disruption to the minimum when working near and around the village, but inevitably the residents nearest the construction work had to put up with dust, noise and vibration for quite a while. The Bedford Southern Bypass was opened in September 1996 after two years construction. It is 8.4 kilometres long and runs from the A421 Kempston Southern Relief Road to the A428 west of the Renhold turn. The Western Bypass which should complement it remains a distant dream.

At the turn of the 20th century there were still fields along the Wilstead Road past Medbury Lane, some of which were purchased for development in later years. On the roadside opposite, and still standing, are two timber framed thatched cottages with adjacent barns. These cottages which appear to be semi-detached are about four hundred years old and according to records were at that time two separate cottages as there was a small gap between them visible only from inside. Sometime, probably around the late 1880s, when the cottages where renovated, the gap was filled in and the thatched roof joined together. Since 1997 one of the cottages has been enlarged and refurbished. A well regarded dressmaker used to live in this cottage over fifty years ago. Next to these cottages is a detached house, which also used to be two cottages.

Further along is Pear Tree Farm which is one of the two remaining farms in the village and part of the Whitbread estate. The present farm house dates from 1882. The tenant farmer is Mr David Hall. The Hall family moved from Old Harrowden in 1957 and lived in Village Farm. In 1971 David Hall took over the tenancy of Pear Tree Farm but the Halls continued to farm land at Village Farm for many years and thus had fields either side of Wilstead Road totalling about 1200 acres. After Mr Hall senior's death in 1983 Village Farm House was let by the Whitbread estate to a succession of tenants. Pear Tree Farm is an arable farm but some years ago was also a dairy farm. There are only 300 acres

Bridge nearly finished   *Photos by Mrs S. King*

Bridge completed and road restored to normal

The fishing lake *(see page 83)*   *Photo by Mrs S. King*

Pear Tree View *(see page 85)*   *Photo by C. Marotta*

left of the farm as a great deal has been used for development purposes. Some of the land north of Medbury Lane was used for one of the borrow pits for the extraction of gravel for the construction of the Bedford Southern Bypass. A conservation lake, a fishing lake owned by the Whitbread estate and leased out, and two car parks were created from the borrow pits. Although a substantial number of shrubs and trees were planted around the site, so far these have not grown sufficiently to seclude the area from the roads.

When archaeological investigations were being carried out for the Bedford Southern Bypass a small Roman farmstead was uncovered near Pear Tree Farm which had apparently occupied the site of a former Iron Age field; several complete pottery and glass vessels were found.

Who would have thought that Elstow would have had a Race Course? But this is so. Horse racing was first held in 1730 and lasted until 1874. The Race Course was on what is known as the "Race Meadows" though no longer meadows but arable. This area was south of the Bedford-Bletchley railway line and west of Ampthill Road. The north western side of the Race Course was next to the railway line so would have been part of the site of the present Interchange Retail Park. There was also a Polo field in this area inside the Race Course loop. Mr Hall farms the majority of the area and on occasions has unearthed remains of the Race Course stand. Maybe a Race Course, or even Polo, would be quite an attraction nowadays!

A Royal Agricultural Show was held on Race Meadows in July 1874, and the tenant farmer supplied turnips and oats for the animals. There was a temporary station between the Midland and London and North Western railway line to enable visitors to the Show to alight at Elstow instead of having to travel to Bedford and back again. The village has also hosted gymkhanas, steam engine rallies and circuses within the area. At the back of Pear Tree Farm, near the railway line, used to be Bedford Gun Club where there was clay pigeon shooting.

In November 1997 Mr Hall lost a whole barn of hay and the blaze could be seen for some distance away. It was a most unfortunate incident but these things do happen at times.

Continuing along Wilstead Road there is a brick built bus shelter which was proposed by the Parish Council in 1974, but it took nearly three years before it was actually constructed.

Before the road bends round and meets the A6, there are seven quite old terraced cottages with good sized back gardens and apparently years ago the residents had pig sties and thus kept pigs. That was probably why that end of the village was referred to as "Bacon End". Along from the cottages is a pre-war bungalow and finally another very old cottage which was one of the other privately owned properties in the village. This cottage has been extended and extensively renovated over recent years.

Some of the residents of these cottages have to park their cars on the roadside as they have no off-the-road parking. Before the right turn from Luton to Elstow was closed to traffic apart from buses, there were several accidents with traffic rounding the bend and bumping into the parked cars, or even landing in the front gardens. Traffic travelling south on the A6 can turn left into the village and very occasionally similar incidents occur. In an endeavour to remedy this problem part of the road opposite the cottages has been widened to enable traffic to pass more easily.

On crossing Wilstead Road from the cottages there is Moss Lane leading to South Avenue, and standing back from a sward of grass, on which stand some lovely chestnut trees, is part of Pear Tree View. The chestnut trees take quite a battering from the local children when the chestnuts are ripe. Whatever do the kids do with all the bags of conkers they collect apart from playing "conkers"?

In 1930 eight council houses, some of which are now privately owned, were built in Moss Lane and a little later other properties were built as far as number 14 South Avenue. Moss Lane is somewhat peculiar as part of the way along it turns left into a short roadway, then bears right thus running at the back of South Avenue and coming to a dead end with just an alleyway leading into South Avenue. The houses on this part of Moss Lane are all on one side only and were built around 1935, although there is one detached house bearing the date 1932 and two post-war detached houses complete the road.

A bungalow on the front part of Moss Lane was built round an Army hut. A butcher used to live in Moss Lane and was a dab hand where pigs were concerned, so anyone wishing to have a pig slaughtered called upon his services.

South Avenue which is an extension of the front part of Moss Lane is a cul-de-sac and the majority of the houses are about fifty years old and have open views across the fields. During the last war, one of the older houses had a shop in the front room and slab cake was a favourite buy. Behind the houses at the bottom of South Avenue is a fox cover and as recently as February 1999 foxes have been seen running across the road. Kingfishers could also be seen in the brook which runs nearby.

In the 1950s the Lynn Farm fields were purchased for development and around 1954 council houses were built on Medbury Lane, part of Pear Tree View and Lynn Close. Most of these houses were tenanted by personnel who had been employed at Cardington Camp. There is one couple still in residence in Lynn Close from those days. Some of the properties, of course, are now privately owned. About a decade later houses were built to form the southern part of Lynn Close and Pear Tree View.

The shop on the corner of Lynn Close and Pear Tree View was built by the developer as a shop with a flat above. Pear Tree Stores has always been a friendly village shop selling groceries, sweets and newspapers, etc. Half day closing used to be on a Tuesday afternoon, now the shop is open seven days a week from 7 a.m. to 7 p.m. and 8 a.m. to 4 p.m. on Sundays.

Pear Tree View has always had a sward of grass in front of the houses, although from Medbury Lane to Lynn Close the grass did not stretch to the footpath on Wilstead Road as there was a ditch. This ditch became quite an eyesore when it was filled with water after heavy rain and overgrown with weeds and cow parsley. Some of the children used to try and ride their bicycles across the ditch which could have been quite dangerous if they had landed on the road. It was felt for some time that the ditch should be filled in but it was only after the opening of the Bedford Southern Bypass that such action became possible. At the instigation of the Elstow Parish Council, Thorburn Colquhoun and Wimpey-Amey agreed, as a gesture to the village, to pipe and fill in the ditch and re-seed the site. Following this, and with the agreement of the Bedford Borough Council, some old elderberry bushes and broken down trees overgrown with ivy, were removed from the site. New trees were planted in the hope that eventually they will correspond with the mature trees on the rest of the Pear Tree View.

At an annual Parish Meeting a few years ago a request was made for some spring bulbs to be planted around the village. After consultation with the Bedford Borough Council it was agreed that daffodil and crocus bulbs could be planted in the grass along Pear Tree View, along by the Sports and Social Centre and other suitable areas. The bulbs were purchased by the Parish Council and a team of residents planted them and very nice they look when in flower, although unfortunately over the years some of the bulbs seem to have disappeared.

The telephone box which stands on Wilstead Road used to be sited at the corner of Moss Lane, but in 1981 it was resited to its present position as it was considered that it would be more convenient for the residents in the area. It seems a shame that the red boxes have been phased out but whatever shape or colour, telephone boxes seem to have an attraction for people who do not need to use them for the purpose for which they are intended.

MEDBURY LANE

At the top of Medbury Lane, which used to be called Medbury Road is Medbury Farm, the other remaining farm in Elstow and part of the Whitbread estate. There was also an old house which centuries ago was probably known as the Manor of Maidbury. The present farm house dates from 1884 and the farm covers about five hundred acres, mostly arable but with grazing for a small flock of ewes. Prior to 1980 it was a dairy farm too.

The Clark family have been tenants since 1928. As well as farming Mr Clark (senior) made rope show halters for shire horses. In the last war he made stretchers for the village's first aid post and when an aeroplane landed in one of his fields, on 23rd December 1944, it was Mr Clark who guarded it until it was checked out as "one of ours" (British). Actually the plane was a Bristol Beaufighter from the 51 OTU Unit at Cranfield which lost power and being unable to maintain height belly landed in the field. Fortunately the two crew members were uninjured. The plane was no doubt dismantled and taken away on long trailers known as "Queen Marys". Medbury Farm also had a line of incendiary bombs dropped across their fields - the enemy presumably looking for Cardington Camp or the Bomb Factory. Two Italian Prisoners of War lived in at the farm and assisted in various ways on the land. Mr Clark (senior) was a sidesman at Elstow Abbey Church and an Elstow Parish Councillor, as is his son today.

The family who used to live in the Manor House emigrated to New Zealand and named their sheep station "Medbury". Their descendants still visit the present farm.

At one time there was a row of seven great walnut trees on Medbury Lane near the farm house but these were cut down during the last war. Many years ago there was a rifle range at the back of the old house. Some years ago a cowman shot himself in some farm buildings which used to stand on Medbury Lane.

The Oakley Foxhouds and the North Bucks Beagles meet and hunt over the land, and each year the Young Farmers hold their annual Shed Shuffle, which has run for thirty-three years, in a big barn at the farm.

The Medbury Brook goes through part of the land as it flows from Wilstead towards Harrowden. There is a right of way across the fields from Medbury Lane to Wilstead which is marked by a blue waymark sign as a Marston Vale Public Bridleway.

The Forest of Marston Vale, originally named Marston Vale Community Forest, is one of twelve Community Forests in England. The Community Forests were initiated in 1989 by the Countryside Agency and the Forestry Commission in response to the national need to diversify land-use. They are intended to give local people the opportunity to enjoy and discover the great outdoors. The Forest of Marston Vale plan proposed to enhance the landscapes and amenities within the Vale whilst conserving its agricultural heritage. Most land in the Vale is private and therefore all waymark signs must be adhered to and all property and woodland respected. The Forest of Marston Vale consists of sixty-one square miles between Bedford and the M1 motorway near Milton Keynes, and has a number of walks, cycle routes and heritage sites to enjoy such as the Moot Hall, Elstow Abbey Church with refreshments available at the Swan Public House at Elstow.

When walking along Medbury Lane now, instead of an expanse of fields, one can see the fishing lake, traffic travelling on the Bedford Southern Bypass and houses on the Abbeyfields development. It is known as progress; never mind the quiet rural environment, but maybe when the trees and shrubs planted round the lakes and along the bypass, mature these "blots" on the landscape will be less conspicuous. There is, however, a fine view of the two hangers at Cardington where the R101 airship was built.

Chapter 9

CHARACTERS

Over the years, Elstow, like many villages, has had some village characters, some with fitting nicknames.

"Swinger" Benson was employed by Bedford Council as the roadman for Elstow. He kept the roads well repaired and painted the white lines on the roads by hand. His grandson still lives in the village.

Joe and Ernie Burr were good gamekeepers. Joe took part in the "Have A Go" programme when Wilfred Pickles recorded the show from Elstow.

"Hoppy" Chambers was a market gardener and Taffy Curtis and his father were gravediggers. Taffy was an old soldier and a recluse but liked his drink.

"Drippy" Draper was the village mole catcher whose nose always seemed to be dripping!

"Wag" Fox was a handyman and was so handy that he ripped the middle out of his house.

Monty Harper was a milkman and his son Charlie used to collect mushrooms and blackberries and took them to the shops for sale.

William Cunningham known as "Hairy Henry" or "Old Henry", was a tramp who had a beard similar to W. G. Grace, the cricketer. He was a nice old man and was quite well educated. He spent about a quarter of a century around the village and worked for the Wagstaffs for eighteen years helping with the threshing, and did gardening for various farmers. He used to travel further afield in the summer and went to London for the Queen's Coronation and assisted with the erection of the stands along the processional route. It is believed that he bathed in the brook but he always had a bucket of hot water from the steam engine for a wash down after work on the farms. Henry generally slept in various barns and fed on rabbits and pigeons etc., but he preferred strong tea to beer. When he was taken ill on a farm in 1957 and later died in hospital, Elstow lost a well loved character.

"Put" Fox was an odd job man and Harry Ingram was a farm labourer who worked on the thatched ricks and always wore a bowler hat when going to Church.

"Dipper" Keep lived in Holly Cottage and used to 'baptise' people in the Elstow brook hence the name "Dipper".

Rosie was a tramp who travelled between Luton and Northampton and slept under the hay in a barn at Lynn Farm when in the neighbourhood.

Charlie Prudden was a well known farmer in the village and was well versed in the history of Elstow. He called a spade a spade but sometimes used more colourful language.

There has been, and still are, a number of good cricketers and footballers in the village. Some years back one late resident was a very good hockey player and was Secretary of the Bedford Hockey Club.

Another past resident worth a mention is Oswald James Crouch who although a printer, also gave piano lessons. He was organist at Lidlington Church and would cycle the ten miles there and back on a Sunday. He also played at St. Pauls Church in Bedford and for services at Bedford Hospital. Mr Crouch was another participant in the "Have A Go" programme.

More than fifty years ago Elstow residents had a variety of occupations, as of course, they do today, they included a bus driver, photographer, school teacher together with hospital, post office and Shire Hall employees.

Peter Pestell, who lived opposite the St. Helena Restaurant, was a well known villager, who devoted much of his life to the history of John Bunyan. Peter could often be found showing people the John Bunyan memorial at Old Harrowden, tending his cottage garden or looking after his beloved Moot Hall, for which he was caretaker for many years, especially during the John Bunyan exhibition. He was ably assisted in this task by his wife Lily. Peter was a gentle caring man, a dedicated Christian, he would help anybody and had time for everyone.

The following poem, written by Barbara Honeysett, a friend of the family for over forty years, goes to show that he was a remarkable man.

This tribute has been dedicated to Peter by Raffaele Marotta, proprietor of the St. Helena, who Peter helped in many ways on numerous occasions.

In Elstow was a godly man
Across the road from here,
In cottage thatched - with wife and boys,
He lived for many a year.

John Bunyan was his favourite saint,
Of him he loved to tell
His holy life, his sayings quaint
His time in prison cell.

Moot Hall was his especial care
And lots of folk he took
To see the many things there shown
And Bunyan's famous book.

It told of how a Christian trod
Along life's varied way
And how he persevered to God
And everlasting day.

The Pilgrim's Progress it is called;
By thousands it's been read;
A help it's been to many folk
The heavenly path to tread.

For pilgrims often go astray
And need to have a Guide
To keep them in the narrow way
With Jesus by their side.

And Peter Pestell followed on,
John Bunyan's way he passed
And now he dwells in perfect peace
In Glory Land at last.

By Barbara Honeysett, a friend of forty years

THIS STONE WAS ERECTED IN THE
FESTIVAL OF BRITAIN YEAR
TO MARK THE BIRTHPLACE OF

JOHN BUNYAN
1628-1688

Peter Pestel

Oswald

William Cunningham, also known as "Old Henry" (see page 88)
Bedfordshire & Luton Archives Services (Bedfordshire Times Collection)

James Crouch with Wilfred Pickles and Mabel (see page 89)

Chapter 10

LACE MAKING

From records of Elstow it is known that lace was made in the village and well over a century ago there was a Lace School, which was held in one of the cottages. Children of the poor attended the school and were taught pillow lace making. The girls were charged 2d (two pence) a week and the boys 4d (four pence); as the boys did not like the work the teachers tried to turn boys into girls, but this caused endless trouble resulting in one lad, goaded by a stroke of the cane, running out of the school and dropping his pillow down the well on the Green. This lad happened to become an uncle of a former resident of Elstow.

In 1973 the Secretary of the Elstow Craft Centre had an idea to hold a "Lace In" at the Centre. This involved the three lace classes getting together for a day after the summer classes had ceased. The event was advertised so that ex-students could join in and it was also broadcast on south west radio with the result that it turned out to be a national rather than a local day. There was an exhibition of lace but none was for sale.

The organisers were amazed at the widespread interest in lace making and so a similar day was organised in 1975. A coach party from Sheffield had to be turned away due to lack of space. On this occasion, sales tables were allowed, supplies from Braggins Departmental Store (Beales took over the site); a glass bobbin maker and a carpenter from Burton Latimer with a number of bobbins exhibited his goods and eventually became a large supplier of lace making equipment worldwide. Mr Braggins used to purchase lace from the Lace School and individual lace makers for sale in the store.

Following these two successful days the Lace Guild was formed with its inaugural meeting at Mander College in April 1976. The Lace Guild, which is worldwide, has a membership of around 6000.

Mrs Sandra King (an Elstow resident), who is a member of the Lace Guild, was involved with the Aragon Lacemakers in the making of a lace picture of Bamberg in May 1982. A year later she was granted permission from Bedford

Borough Council to reproduce the Coat of Arms (Eagle and Castle) in lace. Mrs King then decided, egged on by her husband, to make the picturesque village of Elstow in lace. The Abbey Church, the Moot Hall and Bunyan's Mead along with Bunyan's cottage (the design of which was based on photographs and postcards as the cottage had been demolished) and the Village Sign, were made and as a "complete village" mounted on black felt and framed. A village sign for Elstow had not been contemplated at this time but Mrs King had seen the illustration of the sign in "The Bunyan Country" book and hence was able to make a lace copy. She subsequently made a second copy mounted on maroon cotton fabric as a bible marker for the Elstow Abbey Church and this can be seen on the lectern in the Church.

MISCELLANEOUS

Apparently a Carnival took place in Elstow in the late 1920s as an old poster shows that the fifth Annual Carnival was held on 5th July 1930 in the Abbey Ruins when a Royal Air Force Gymnastic Display and Band were amongst the attractions. Some residents remember that these Carnivals had the wooden revolving "horse", you know, whereby participants had to sit on the back of the object and move gently forward towards the head before the "horse" revolved and threw them off.

Around 1910 there was a bus between Goldington Green and Elstow, this ceased in May 1913 but later in the year Elstow was included in the Hitchin circular route. The Eastern National Omnibus Company ran a regular two hourly bus service through the village from Bedford to Luton and return from about 1929 to 1950. They were double decker buses, probably Leyland TD1 or AEC Regent, and of course, all buses had bus conductors in those days. The United Counties Omnibus Company took over the bus service in 1951/52. There was also a bus which did a circular route from Bedford to Elstow and Clapham. This bus ran hourly and used to turn at West End, near the post office, where it stopped for a twenty minute break - imagine trying to do such a turn nowadays! Since September 1998 Elstow has been lucky in having a half hourly bus service, the X52 travels from Bedford to Luton and return, whilst service 144 travels through the village from Flitwick to Bedford and back (for part of the day this service takes in the Bedford South Wing Hospital which is

useful for people with hospital appointments). The bus fare from Elstow to Bedford used to be two pence (2d) today it is 95p - what an increase over the years!

Coming into Elstow there was a bus stop on the High Street as today, one where the Bedford Southern Bypass bridge is and another on the corner of Moss Lane; the latter two have been replaced by one on Wilstead Road opposite the bus shelter. Going into Bedford there were two bus stops, the bus shelter on Wilstead Road and near the post office.

To celebrate King George V Silver Jubilee in 1935, all Elstow residents over sixty-five years of age were given a new Jubilee half crown. The school children had a special tea in the school and those under school age had a tea with their mothers in the Church Hall. Mr Whitbread donated £20 towards the expenses and a house to house collection was also made thus enabling the residents to have a special meat tea.

For the Coronation in 1937 the elderly folk received a new half crown specially minted for the Coronation. To celebrate the Peace in 1945 there were sports for the children followed by a social in the evening for both children and adults. As in 1935 a house to house collection was made towards the necessary expenses and the same method of raising funds was used in 1953 when Elstow celebrated the Coronation of our present Queen with a special tea in the school for all residents.

The Bright Hour was formed in 1937 by the then Vicar's wife as a social gathering on a Tuesday afternoon for ladies of the village. Over the years the Bright Hour raised a great deal of money for various charities. Amongst other things members held jumble sales and gave a party each year for the Senior Citizens. To celebrate their 40th anniversary in 1977 the members of the Bright Hour donated a seat to the Church which was placed by the Bell Tower. At one time there were up to fifty members but in the mid-nineties membership had fallen to less then ten, so unfortunately the Bright Hour faded away in 1998 when a pair of candlesticks, obtained from the remaining funds, were presented to the Church.

There used to be a regular police patrol in the village and one of the policeman responsible for Elstow lived in Wilstead. This particular policeman had a habit of appearing from nowhere and would give the lads and lasses a telling off for some misdemeanour which he had seen and which sometimes resulted in a visit to the parents too. He always had time for a brief chat with the village folk and was indeed a well liked and respected "Bobby". How times have changed! - two police officers are responsible for Elstow now but apparently have to be summoned when required.

On 3rd September 1939 about fifteen evacuees from London, accompanied by two foster mothers, arrived in Elstow from London Council controlled Homes. The children and the foster mothers were billeted around the village and Edward Bowen, known as "Curly" was one who never returned to London. He remembers sitting in the school on arrival from London whilst the Elstow residents decided which boy or girl they would have to look after. What an ordeal it must have been for the tired and, no doubt, frightened children. "Curly" lived with a very loving family and helped around the village. He worked for Charlie Prudden and as a beater for the Shoots from Elstow Lodge, he eventually became a Post Office employee. Although he moved to Millar Road for a few years, he returned to his present house in West End and is well known in the village. "Curly" can remember who lived in all the old houses in the village and what they did for a living. He was impressed by the great atmosphere in the village in those days with everyone joining in the various activities, and he was intrigued by the curious method of numbering the houses. Another evacuee still pays visits to friends she made in Elstow.

The unusual numbering of the old cottages is how they appear in the Whitbread Estate Register, although some cottages were built prior to the Whitbreads' acquisition of Elstow they were presumably given a number at that time. The cottages on the High Street were from 171 to 191 which was the house by the bridge over the Elstow brook. On the opposite side of the road from Pear Tree Farm down to the Post Office there was 198 to 206. The Church End cottages were 207 to 214, with one side of West End 215 to 218 and the other side 219 to 233. Why did the Elstow numbers start so high? - well maybe because some of the cottages at Southill were numbered from 33 to 68, houses on the corner of Harrowden Lane were 269 to 271 and two houses on Cardington Green were 320 and 322, it would seem therefore that Elstow came in between!

The majority of the numbers are still current although the High Street cottage numbers finish at 174 as the Bunyan's Mead numbers replaced the rest of the High Street thus the house by the bridge is now 28 Bunyan's Mead. The new private cottage homes on the High Street go from 152 to 160 and other 20th century houses, not owned by the Whitbread estate, also seem to have a rather irregular numbering system. Medbury Lane houses all have even numbers whereas Lynn Close, South Avenue, Wigram Close along with Hillesden Avenue and roads there off have odd numbers on one side and even on the other. In most of the other roads the house numbers run consecutively apart from the cottages at the far end of the village on Wilstead Road which are all named and not numbered. It must be quite a headache for the postman/lady and other trades people to find the correct address!

Prior to 1939 a van with paraffin and oil used to visit the village as did a horse drawn fish and chip van which stopped at The Swan and a bag of chips was one penny. Shortly after the war, various tradesmen visited on a regular basis - there was the linen van from Turvey, a paraffin and soap van, a cake man who sold six cakes for sixpence, two bread vans, fresh fish could be purchased from a fish man with a bicycle, and of course, there was a Walls Stop Me and Buy One ice cream tricycle. What a shame these services had to cease! Since 1980 the mobile library service has been calling at Elstow every fortnight on a Wednesday stopping in the High Street and Pear Tree View, and an ice cream van comes round occasionally.

In August 1941 an Invasion Committee was set up in Elstow and met regularly until the end of the war in 1945. Residents volunteered for fire watching duties, there were A.R.P. wardens (Air-raid precautions) and a First Aid Officer. Mr Clark (senior) made stretchers, he supplied the poles and the necessary material was obtained from money raised by members of the Bright Hour.

Also during the last war, a large tree which stood near the present Bunyan's Mead telephone box, had the trunk painted white to prevent people walking into it in the blackout.

A highway offence was recorded in 1824 whereby one Sam Foxley was convicted and fined £1.5s (one pound five shillings) for riding his wagon loaded with coal on the turnpike road between Bedford and Woburn at Elstow, for not having a person on foot or on horseback to guide him.

Years ago anyone in the village spotted by the local policeman riding a bicycle without lights was subjected to a fine.

Various accidents, some unfortunately fatal, have occurred in the village. As far back as 1862 a boy of fourteen years was killed when he fell from a farm cart and about fifty years ago a resident died in a house fire. In October 1944 an American Airman of the 92nd Bomb Group was returning from a visit to friends in St. Albans and accepted a lift in a lorry which was forced off the road in Elstow and hit Bunyan's cottage killing the officer. The lorry was understood to be a brewery lorry as a resident of the village who was a pupil at the Elstow school at the time, remembers being taken out of school, by the headmaster, along with other boys to see the incident and recalls beer barrels being scattered about the road. For several years now, Elstow has had a 30 mph speed limit throughout the village, although unfortunately, it is not always adhered to, and there is a Heavy Goods Vehicle Limit on West End, High Street and Wilstead Road.

In the severe winter of 1947 the Elstow brook froze and the snow was six feet deep in places. One villager remembers that about 1949 a whirlwind struck the village, it blew slates off the school and houses in Medbury Lane, severely damaged the roof of a barn at the back of the Red Lion and even snapped off the tops of some apple trees in the gardens along the High Street.

In the 1950s a Best Kept Village Competition was organised by the Bedfordshire Association of Parish Councils and sponsored by Calor Gas. There was a prize for small, medium and large sized villages with a special prize for some particular village feature. The Judges visited the villages who had entered the competition, unannounced generally in July and made general comments. Elstow came third in the medium sized village category in 1963 and 1968 and first in 1986 being awarded a cup and also an Acer tree for the playing field. There is now a Village of the Year Competition sponsored by the Daily Telegraph and Calor Gas with money prizes to spend on community projects, the categories being varied such as Communicating with the Parish.

All the old cottages, of course, had outside toilets with buckets or earth closets. As time passed installation of inside toilets, and construction of sewers were considered but met with some controversy as part of the village wanted street lighting. However, a sewerage system was eventually provided around 1965.

The first street lamp in the village was erected near the Red Lion with others following the development of Bunyan's Mead. There are, however, still no street lights beyond the bridge although the topic has been raised on occasions it seems that the majority of residents at the far end of the village are against street lighting. Here again at this end of the village there is no gas, so residents, in the main, use electricity for cooking, and oil or solid fuel for heating. Installation of gas would be quite expensive and residential surveys by the Gas Company over the years have had little response. It is a nuisance for residents though when there is an electricity power failure, as in most instances, it is not even possible to boil a kettle.

There are two notice boards in the village, one by the Post Office and one on the wall of the Pear Tree Stores, both are owned by the Elstow Parish Council. It is understood that a notice board is to be erected on Hillesden Avenue and another on the Abbeyfields estate, this one to be financed by the developer.

The John Bunyan Trail which was created by the Ramblers Association (Beds. Area) as a contribution to their 60th Jubilee celebrations and dedicated to the memory of John Bunyan covers approximately seventy-five miles. Section One which begins at Sundon Country Park takes in Ampthill, Cranfield and Bromham before finishing at Elstow is about forty-five miles; whilst Section Two which starts at the Moot Hall at Elstow and includes Shefford and Barton-le-Clay finishes after around twenty-five miles at Sundon Hills which are reputed to be John Bunyan's delectable mountains in The Pilgrim's Progress. Most of the route is marked by special Bunyan Trail waymark discs and an information panel regarding the Trail is on the Bedfordshire County Council Leisure Services Department notice board by the Moot Hall. (Leaflets are available from the Bedford Tourist Information Office).

Some quilters in Bedfordshire were involved in the making of a Millennium quilt depicting various scenes of Bedford and surrounding villages. The quilters were supplied with a sky blue fabric and a green grass fabric but had to obtain any other colours they required. The work was mostly appliqué with some surface embroidery and had three panels, the middle panel approximately 7ft long by 3ft wide with a small panel on either side measuring 5ft long by 2ft wide. The quilt was made up of various size blocks and when the basic shape arrived at Bedford only small blocks were left. Sandra King, from the village, decided to do the Moot Hall on her block. The finished quilt was on show at the Bedfordshire Millennium Festival held at Shuttleworth College between 28th and 30th August 1999 but where it will finally be hung is not known.

Chapter 11

THE PARISH COUNCIL

The majority of Parish Councils were created by an Act of Parliament in 1894. Prior to this there were what were known as Vestry meetings which dealt with all matters concerning the village and as a rule the Vicar of the parish acted as Chairman. Once the Parish Councils were formed they undertook all the civil matters whilst the Vestry meetings continued as an ecclesiastical body until 1922 when all affairs of the Church were transferred to newly established Parochial Church Councils.

Most small towns and villages in England have Parish Councils. A Parish Council is an organ of local opinion, various authorities consult Parish Councils because they are in closer and regular contact with the electorate, whereas these other authorities are further removed.

The Local Government Act of 1972 regarding Local Government Re-organisation, which became effective on 1st April 1974, redefined and modernised Parish Councils giving them many new powers and rights, one important item being to notify Parish Councils of all planning applications within their areas.

A Parish Council acts within the framework of legislation conferred upon it by Parliament and its functions are mainly discretionary. In its role as an executive body the Parish Council has many statutory functions and as the elected body of the parish has the power of decision. The Parish Council is able to voice the views of the residents on many issues, such as making representations in regard to sensitive planning applications. A natural role for the Parish Council is to take a lead on issues affecting interests in the area as it generally has initial access to local information, resources and capability to act.

A Parish Council must meet at least three times a year and hold a Parish Meeting annually for all electors of the parish. Meetings are not allowed to be held on licensed premises.

The National Association of Local Councils provides Parish Councils with advice on legal and procedural matters concerning individual Councils. The County Association of Local Councils is designed to meet the needs of Parish Councils with the help of the National Association. It has specialised knowledge to answer queries on a variety of topics and also arranges courses for Parish Councillors and Clerks. The secretariat for the County Association, in the majority of cases, is provided by the County Rural Community Councils which are voluntary organisations, some having been in existence since the mid-1920s. They have a wide range of contacts and knowledge of local activities.

The number of Parish Councillors on a Parish Council varies according to the population of the village. Parish Councillors, who have to be residents of the parish, are elected by the parish electorate for a period of four years, but can stand for re-election. They receive no remuneration for their services but are allowed to claim for travelling expenses incurred for an approved duty outside the parish. A Parish Council Chairman is elected annually by the Parish Councillors. The Clerk, however, who need not reside in the parish, is selected for office by interview and is paid by the Parish Council and can continue in office for as long as he, or she, wishes subject to the satisfaction of the Parish Council. It is helpful if the Clerk has a knowledge of meeting routine, record and Minutes keeping and general Council matters.

With regard to Elstow Parish Council records show that the first Parish Meeting was held in the Elstow School on 4th December 1894 for the purpose of electing seven Parish Councillors. The first Parish Council meeting was on 31st December 1894. There are still seven Parish Councillors and meetings these days are held in the Committee Room of the Sports and Social Centre. Elections are linked with the County and Borough Council elections and are held on the same day, with a separate voting paper for the proposed Councillors.

As is the general role of the Parish Council, Elstow Parish Council is the elected representative of the village and as such decides on projects best suited to the village. It considers planning applications relevant to Elstow though the views expressed are not always accepted by the Planning Committee of Bedford Borough Council who make the final decision. The Parish Council endeavours to act upon requests and complaints from residents wherever possible. If the matter is beyond them it is referred to the appropriate authorities. Elstow Parish Council also liaises with developers and contractors regarding new roads and housing developments, and keeps a look out for potholes in the roads around the village, and damage to public property such as telephone boxes, so that the proper authorities can be notified and repairs undertaken as soon as possible. Over the last decade Elstow Parish Council has had meetings about every couple of months as there has been a vast amount of business to discuss mostly due to the construction of the new housing developments and the Bedford Southern Bypass. A meeting lasts about two hours depending on the amount of business and attendance by the Councillors is in general very good. The County Councillor and Borough Councillor for Elstow attend some of the meetings.

The Parish Council precept which is paid annually (by the Bedford Borough Council) is enforceable by order of the Secretary of State and is a sum required to meet expenses of the Parish Council, is chargeable separate on its area and payable by all council tax payers.

During its existence Elstow Parish Council has had some long standing Chairpersons and Councillors. Two present Councillors have served for over sixteen years and over the years the Clerks to the Elstow Parish Council have held office for twelve years or more.

Although a small Parish Council, Elstow Parish Council seems to be well thought of by both Bedfordshire County Council and Bedford Borough Council and also by the County and National Association of Parish Councils. Little but good!

Chapter 12

THE ELSTOW POORS ESTATE

The Elstow Poors Estate is a registered Charity and according to the Charity Commissioners for England and Wales was reported in the Printed Reports of the Former Commissioners for Inquiring Concerning Charities published in 1882. It advised that the Poors Estate was under the management of the Churchwardens and Overseers of the poor of the parish. Rents for some arable land at Elstow, Kempston and Wilshamstead were received by the Charity each Christmas. Part of the money was used for the purchase of bread, a small loaf being given each Sunday, from Christmas to Easter, to poor widows who resided within the parish of Elstow. The rest of the money was distributed at Christmas amongst the poor of the parish, including widows, according to a list of beneficiaries previously agreed. The records show that in 1884, 371 persons received one shilling and tenpence per head and the bread cost nearly £4, the actual number of loaves purchased was not quoted. Over the years the cash amounts and numbers fluctuated.

At the first Parish Meeting held in 1894 details concerning the finances of the Poors Estate were recorded and a financial statement has been presented to the Elstow Annual Parish Meeting ever since.

Section 14 of the Local Government Act of 1894 replaced Churchwardens and Overseers by four Trustees appointed by the Parish Council and this was restated in a section of the Charities Act 1960, though there were no rules as to the actual composition of the Trustee body. There are four Trustees who administer the monies of the Elstow Poors Estate.

Around the 1950s some of the arable land was sold pursuant to an Order of the Commissioners and proceeds invested in Government Consolidated Stock in the name of the official custodian for Charities whereby a dividend was paid every six months. The investment service was abolished under the Charities Act of 1972, so the Trustees placed the balance of the monies into another account.

In 1975 the Trustees decided that the distribution of bread should cease due to the increased cost in relation to the static income of the Charity. Two years later it was agreed that future beneficiaries of the monetary Christmas gift should be widows and old age pensioners who had lived in the Civil Parish of Elstow continuously for over ten years.

The particulars of the Elstow Poors Estate are given in the Central Register of Charities. For over fifty years the Objects showed "Bread for widows and needy spinsters and cash distribution for Old Age Pensioners". In 1992 the then Trustees resolved that the Objects of the Charity should be modified to fulfill the requirements of Section 2 of the 1985 Charities Act, so the Objects description now states:- "For the relief of persons resident in the Civil Parish of Elstow who are in need, hardship or distress, in gifts of kind or grants of money (which may include grants to any almshouse or other charitable institution established for the benefit of persons qualified as aforesaid): provided that income shall not be applied directly in relief of rates, taxes or other public funds but may be applied in supplementary relief or assistance provided out of public funds".

The Elstow Poors Estate still has some land at Wilstead which is rented to a local farmer, this money goes towards the amount paid out for the monetary Christmas gift.

The Trustees meet in private once a year, unless there is any urgent business to discuss, to decide upon the amount of the Christmas money and consider any new applications. In the late 1990s there were about thirty beneficiaries and the expenditure in the region of £300. Each year a notice is placed on the village noticeboards so that any single pensioners or married couples, both of whom are in receipt of the State pension, and have lived in the village of Elstow for more than ten years, may apply for consideration of the Christmas gift if they consider themselves eligible.

The Elstow Poors Estate has never had a substantial amount of cash, and this is certainly the case at present but the Trustees hope to continue to give a small monetary gift at Christmas to those eligible, for as long as possible, and they will also consider any request for assistance provided the Objects of the Charity are met.

Chapter 13

BOMB FACTORY

During the Second World War there was a Royal Ordnance Factory, otherwise known as the bomb factory, on the site of the present Elstow Storage Depot. What had this to do with Elstow? Maybe not a lot; but at least one resident of Elstow was employed at the factory in the administration office.

The factory, which was managed by J. Lyons & Co. of Cadbury Hall, London, for the Ministry of Supply, opened in February 1942 and by July 4000 pound bombs and mortar shells were being produced. Later 2000 pound bombs for the Royal Air Force and 'A' mines for the Royal Navy were made. It was mostly women and girls who filled the bombs.

The factory was a completely self contained complex under, of course, the tightest security. It had its own roads, railway, power plants and workshops. Amongst the facilities were canteens, a post office, a laundry and a chemist, along with a medical service with a doctor and nursing staff. There was also a Chaplain, fire brigade and police, with offices and clerical staff as well as a welfare department to help all workers with any staff or domestic problems. Thousands of staff were employed twenty-four hours a day, many were billeted around Bedford. Lyons loaned some of their own personnel who had requisite qualifications.

In May 1943 a section of the factory was equipped as a shell reconditioning depot and thousands of shells of all sizes, and ammunition boxes, were reconditioned and distributed to the war front between July 1943 and June 1945.

Only one fatal accident was recorded in the factory's history. The factory was held in high esteem by the Forces Inspection Department as the percentage of work was amongst the highest in the country.

NIREX

In the early 1980s Elstow residents received a great shock when there was talk of a possible nuclear dump on the site of the Elstow Storage Depot. Although a short distance from Elstow village, the residents were naturally deeply concerned as were thousands of people in Bedford and surrounding areas. Other sites in Essex, Lincolnshire and Humberside had been suggested but that was no help to Elstow.

It appeared that low level radioactive waste was being disposed of at a facility in Cumbria but as this was becoming full Britain required a new national low level disposal facility and this need was one reason for the establishment of Nirex. In 1986 planning permission was given by the Government by Special Development Order for detailed investigation of each site with a full public inquiry to follow any application to develop a low waste facility. Later Nirex decided that a safe near surface disposal facility could be developed at any of the sites but were advised that it would be preferable to develop a multi purpose deep site for both low level and intermediate level radioactive waste than proceed with investigations for a near surface resporitory. Eventually studies were undertaken regarding the possibility of a deep mine or resporitory under the sea bed and Nirex withdrew from all four sites to the great relief of Elstow and no doubt to the residents near the other suggested sites.

Nirex had had guidelines to minimise the risk of any adverse impact that any nuclear dump should have no more than 100,000 people within a five mile radius but the proposed site near Elstow had 120,000.

The suggestion of a nuclear dump near Elstow had an adverse affect on house sales in the village, as no one really wished to live in an area where there might be a nuclear dump.

Bedford, surrounding villages and local authorities were all against such a proposal and the Bedfordshire Against Nuclear Dumping, known as BAND, was formed and worked hard to oppose the proposal. Elstow residents did all in their power with meetings, signing petitions and supporting BAND to express their opposition to such a dump, and won. Bedford launched a petition and in March 1986, 9500 signatures was given to Sir Nicholas Lyell, Q.C., M.P.

for presentation to the House of Commons. Protesters barred the way to the site day and night and commemorative stone was erected on the site and can still be seen.

In 1985 there was a dump at La Hague in France which was then the only place in Europe that bore any similarity to the one proposed for the Elstow area. So, in the July, whilst discussions were maintained and concerns continued to be expressed, Nirex allowed five people from the area to fly on a chartered flight from Luton for a first hand look at the way low level nuclear waste was disposed of there. Three residents from Elstow, one from Wilstead and one from Houghton Conquest went on the day's visit. Of course all were concerned about the prospects of living near a nuclear dump and after their visit were still concerned as the dump site in France was virtually unpopulated, whereas the proposed site at Elstow Storage Depot would be close to a densely populated area.

Horror of horrors, the name Nirex has been heard again, and though times change, surely the opposition would be just as great if not greater, if the name Elstow was even remotely mentioned. The chances of the idea of low level waste disposal proposals being raised again at Elstow are now remote as proposals for a new housing settlement on the site of the Elstow Storage Depot effectively rules out the land availability, which was one reason Elstow was originally proposed. Thank goodness!

LANDFILL SITE

At the top of Wilstead Road on the A6 is a Landfill Site (Waste Disposal Tip) formerly a clay quarry. Sometimes in the summer if the waste had not been covered promptly unpleasant smells permeated throughout the village and flies could be a problem in the houses. There were, however, two representatives from the Elstow Parish Council on the liaison Committee concerning the Landfill Site and they could report such problems direct to the management.

In 1881 at Fletton near Peterborough it was discovered that below the top callow of the Oxford Clay was shale-like, grey-green clay deposit, known as "knotts" and this proved ideal for the making of what became known as Fletton bricks. The "knotts" had four characteristics, one being that the moisture content was constant thus allowing the clay to be crushed into a granular form which could be pressed into a brick shape and fired immediately without having to wait for the green bricks to be cured.

In Bedfordshire the Oxford Clay is exposed over about a twenty square mile area to the south of Bedford. The discovery of the "knotts" was a revolution which outdated the traditional brickworks and turned Bedfordshire into a major brick making centre. It was, therefore, in 1897 that B. J. Forder and Son opened the Fletton brickworks at Elstow southwest of the village and east of the Bedford to London railway line near where the Asphalt Plant is today. The brickworks had its own two foot gauge railway and five chimneys. Due to the decline of brick production during the First World War and the slow recovery afterwards, Forder merged with the London Brick Company in 1923. However, Elstow brickworks continued and in 1973 produced twenty-six million bricks, but unfortunately it closed the same year, and all the chimneys were demolished five years later.

Elstow Pit was developed in the early 1920s on the brickworks site for brick making clay and by 1969 workings had extended north and southwest to the A6. Tipping started on land to the west of the A6 where an access to the Landfill Site was formed. By 1986 much of the pit to the west and northwest had been infilled, clay capped and landscaped. It is understood that until about 1974 tipping was more or less unrestricted as little planning controls existed and no records were required, but since that time tipping has consisted of largely domestic waste. In 1979 Bedfordshire County Council purchased part of the site complex from London Brick Company and a further subsequent area in 1981 thus the County Council operated the Landfill Site which closed in 1998 and is gradually being recapped with clay and two metres of soil to seal it with a view to restoring the site to woodland with open spaces.

Since 4th October 1998 the site adjacent to the Landfill Site has been a Transfer Station and Materials Recycling Facility. Most residents in Bedfordshire have orange plastic sacks, along with their wheeled bins, in which to put newspapers, cans and plastic bottles for recycling. The dust cart is emptied at the Transfer Station where the orange sacks are extracted; the rest of the rubbish is then conveyed by articulated vehicles to the Landfill Site at Stewartby. The contents of the orange sacks travel on a conveyor belt and are sorted by hand and segregated into different bins. The cans and plastic bottles are flattened by machine and baled for transportation to relevant manufacturers for recycling, whilst the newspapers are bulked to a storage area. The orange sacks are also recycled. There are twenty-five employees on the site who work from 8 a.m. to 5 p.m. Monday to Friday. When the Recycling Facility becomes busier no doubt longer hours or shift work will be considered.

The office building of the Materials Recycling Facility has an Education Room where visiting parties of school children can see how recycling works. The centre caters for about one hundred children a week from all Bedfordshire schools. Open Days are held occasionally to enable members of the public to see round the site.

It is amazing what can be recycled - twenty-four Cola bottles make a fleece jacket and a vending cup makes a pencil.

The Future

What one wonders will the year 2000 and beyond hold for Elstow? It is known that more development is planned for the future - namely - the barns at Village Farm are to be made into three dwellings and it is proposed that a barn at Lynn Farm be refurbished along with the construction of four bungalows. There is talk of a large food store to be built near the Abbey Middle School, and a Little Chef and Travelodge is expected to be constructed on the A6 near the B.P. Petrol Station by the Bedford Southern Bypass. There are plans for the construction of 4500 dwellings on the Elstow Storage Depot site, together with some re-alignment of the A6, thus creating a self-contained settlement probably to be known as Elstow Village Gardens.

Elstow celebrated the Millennium, which marked the 2000th anniversary of the birth of Jesus Christ, by holding a Millennium party in the Sports and Social Centre on New Year's Eve. This concluded with a torchlight procession to Elstow Abbey Church where people gathered on the Green and lit their Millennium candles as the bells of the church rang in the year 2000 and the Bell Tower was floodlit. A short service followed and the Millennium resolution said -

> "Let there be respect for the earth
> Peace for its people,
> Love in our lives,
> Delight in the good,
> Forgiveness for past wrongs
> And from now on a new start."

Along with churches countrywide Elstow Abbey bells rang out at noon on New Year's Day.

Elstow Parish Council gave a Millennium medal to all children aged 16 and under who lived in the parish.

As a sign of the times some information about Elstow is already on the internet and no doubt more will be added in the future.

Unfortunately many village shops are having to close because they are finding it difficult to compete with the changing shopping habits - supermarkets and the internet. It is to be hoped that here in Elstow the Post Office and the Pear Tree Stores will be able to continue to serve the residents for many years to come.

Let us hope that the village of Elstow will be able to keep its rural identity in the future, which has been the wish of the residents over the years.